INFINITE THINGS TO DO IN RETIREMENT

Discovering Gold in Your Golden Years Without a Pickaxe

BOBBY SUNRAY

© Copyright 2023 - All rights reserved.

The content contained within this book may not be reproduced, duplicated or transmitted without direct written permission from the author or the publisher.

Under no circumstances will any blame or legal responsibility be held against the publisher, or author, for any damages, reparation, or monetary loss due to the information contained within this book, either directly or indirectly.

Legal Notice:

This book is copyright protected. It is only for personal use. You cannot amend, distribute, sell, use, quote or paraphrase any part, or the content within this book, without the consent of the author or publisher.

Disclaimer Notice:

Please note the information contained within this document is for educational and entertainment purposes only. All effort has been executed to present accurate, up to date, reliable, complete information. No warranties of any kind are declared or implied. Readers acknowledge that the author is not engaged in the rendering of legal, financial, medical or professional advice. The content within this book has been derived from various sources. Please consult a licensed professional before attempting any techniques outlined in this book.

By reading this document, the reader agrees that under no circumstances is the author responsible for any losses, direct or indirect, that are incurred as a result of the use of the information contained within this document, including, but not limited to, errors, omissions, or inaccuracies.

Meet the Mastermind Behind the Mirth

Bobby Sunray is not just an author; he is a retired time traveler who has chosen to explore the present rather than the past or the future. Growing up in the United States, Bobby worked in a variety of fields from marketing to engineering. It was not until he retired that he discovered his true passion: living each day as if it were a new adventure.

After finally turning off his alarm clock and saying goodbye to endless work meetings for the last time, Bobby embarked on a journey to find the most authentic and profound experiences life has to offer. He spent a morning getting lost in the narrow streets of Naples in search of the perfect coffee, and devoted entire weeks to exploring postcard-perfect Italian villages. He took up geocaching, organized world dinners with friends, and, incredibly, became something of a rock star in his church choir.

Along the way, Bobby met many retired people, each with a fascinating story to tell. These meetings confirmed to him that retirement was not an end, but an exciting new chapter. With that in mind, he decided to put his adventures and lessons to paper, with the goal of inspiring others to experience retirement with the same enthusiasm.

When not immersed in writing or discovering new hobbies, Bobby enjoys spending time with his family, tending to his rooftop garden, and volunteering in his community. For him, *Infinite Fun Things to Do in Retirement* is not just a book, but a personal journal, a tribute to the art of living each moment to the fullest, and a testament to the fact that you can always reinvent yourself, no matter what your age.

Table of Contents

READY, SET... RETIREMENT! 9

1. THE ART OF "BEING" ...BEFORE VENTURING INTO "DOING" 11
Searching for an Old Self... That Was Younger 12
Age? It's Just a Number You Lose Track Of 14

2. ETERNAL SPRINGTIME IN THE MIND 17
Passions So Hidden They Surprise Everyone 18
From the Chair to the Classroom: Just Be Awake to Learn 20
Neighborhood Tours Like Safaris 22
Board Games: When Monopoly Comes to Life 24

3. HOBBIES: HIDDEN SURPRISES IN EVERYDAY LIFE 27
Terrace Gardening: The Sky Is the Limit 28
Sports: Where Experience Beats Young Legs 30
Creativity: From Quirky Sweaters to Artistic Selfies 32
Rock Stars in the Church Choir 38
Backyard Astrology: Easier Than Astronomy 40

4. PLACES THAT GOOGLE MAPS IS STILL LOOKING FOR 43
Off the Beaten Path Destinations 44
Italy: Postcard Villages Without Postcards 46
In Search of Coffee... Anytime, Anyhow! 49
The World in a Box: Geocaching 50
Themed Journeys: From Sherlock Holmes to Mummies 52
Backpacking: A Borderless Retirement 54

5. DISHES, GLASSES, AND OCCASIONAL MESSES 57
Flavors From Around the World... And From Your Home Bakery 58
Recipes With Anecdotes and Oil Stains 59
From Vine to Glass: An Ethyl Tour 63

Themed Dinners: A World Tour in 80 Dishes 65

6. RELATIONSHIPS: THE TRUE ELIXIR OF LONGEVITY 67
Clubs: For Those Who Are Bored of Being Alone 68

Telling Jokes - And True Stories, Too.. 70

New, Old, Borrowed Friends... 72

7. MONEY WITH A DASH OF CUNNING 75
Make Your Wallet Smile 76

Invest Like a Smart Grandfather 78

When Passion Turns to Profit... 80

Budgets Without Scales 82

8. FIT, ALTHOUGH ROUND IS A FIT 85
Puzzles and Crosswords: The Gym of the Mind 86

Dance and Yoga: Bending Without Breaking 88

Healthy Eating: More Enjoyment, Less Dieting 89

Meditation: Silence - Time to Clear Your Mind!.. 91

9. THE DIGITAL: A DOMESTICATED WORLD 95
Navigating the Web Without Getting Shipwrecked 96

Social Networks: Jokes and Pictures of Cats.. 97

Apps: Little Helpers Hidden in Your Phone 99

10. LEAVE A FOOTPRINT (WITHOUT MAKING A MESS) 103
Writing Memories, Even Fictional Ones 104

DIY: Everything Deserves a Second Life 105

Making Plans, Even Without a Plan.. 107

Renaissance of the Retiree: From Sage to Guide... 109

THE END? JUST A NEW BEGINNING! 111

A TIP OF THE HAT AND YOUR TWO CENTS 113

XX. UNCOVER THE TREASURE 115

Ready, Set... Retirement!

Ah, retirement! The word that for years has seemed synonymous with peace and quiet, long afternoons spent soaking up the sun, maybe a few adventures in faraway places, or maybe just a well-deserved break from the daily grind. But if you think retiring means lounging in your slippers in front of the TV, my friend, you are in for a surprise!

The Day Retirement Turns Out to Be a Surprisingly Young Companion

Have you ever thought of retirement as the classmate you never noticed until he or she revealed a hidden talent during the end-of-year show? That's right. You may have thought of retirement as a long afternoon nap, but it is really an awakening.

The first day of retirement may seem strange. You may wake up at the usual time, perhaps expecting your usual smartphone alarm clock. But when you open your eyes, there is no rush. No meetings to get to, no urgent emails to check. Just sweet nothingness. Or so it seems.

But like a kid in a candy store, you soon realize you are facing a world of possibilities. You can do all the things you've always wanted to do but never had the time. Retirement turns out to be the box of toys you forgot you had.

You have the freedom to rediscover yourself, your passions, and unexpectedly realize that the word "retired" does not mean "old." No, on the contrary! Being retired can mean being younger than ever. Because now you have the time, the energy (yes, still!), and hopefully even some resources to devote to new adventures.

And believe me, you are not alone in feeling this way. Millions of people are finding that retirement is an opportunity to turn over a new leaf. Whether it's traveling, learning a new skill, volunteering, or becoming a master chef in the kitchen, retirement can be the most active and exciting time of your life.

Remember, if you don't worry about getting old, you won't be old. So instead of thinking of retirement as the twilight of life, think of it as a bright dawn, ready to brighten a day full of new adventures.

So, pull yourself out of that chair, kick off your slippers, and get ready to explore the wonderful world of retirement. It's time to live, laugh, and love like never before. Ready, set... retirement!

1. The Art of "Being" ...Before Venturing Into "Doing"

Remember when you were a child and could spend hours looking at clouds, imagining shapes and stories without a care in the world? The beauty of those moments was simply "being." We were present, immersed in the moment, without the desperate need to do. But somewhere along the way, as adults, we became slaves to doing. Our identity became a list of things to do and goals to achieve.

But now, my friend, it is time to rediscover the art of "being."

Before you rush headlong into the myriad of activities and projects you have to do in retirement, take a moment. Take a breath. Look inside yourself. This time in your life offers a unique opportunity: to reconnect with yourself, to discover who you really are when you are not defined by a job or a role.

And if you think this sounds too philosophical, think of it like this: before you build a house, you need a solid foundation. Before you decide how you want to spend your retirement days, it is important to have a clear understanding of what makes you happy, what motivates you, what you are truly passionate about.

Sometimes, in silence and reflection, we can find answers that we have searched for in vain in the hustle and bustle of daily life. You may discover that you really want to travel the world. Or you may discover that you have a hidden passion for painting, writing, or dancing.

The point is, before you venture into the outer world of "doing," immerse yourself in the inner world of "being." Only then will you be truly ready to take advantage of all the wonderful opportunities retirement has to offer. And as you will discover, the possibilities are truly endless. Before you do, learn to be. Your soul will thank you.

Searching for an Old Self... That Was Younger

At the heart of every retiree is a rebellious child with a briefcase, dreaming of returning to his childhood adventures. And when we stop to think about it, we realize that retirement is the ideal opportunity to recapture the daring young man we were.

Think back to your youth. Do you remember those moments when you felt indomitable, invincible, and above all, endlessly curious? Your mind was not stifled by rigid structures or responsibilities; it was a vast ocean of possibilities. Well, who said those days were over? Who decided that as we age, we must give up exploration, experimentation, and the sheer joy of living?

Retirement is not the end; it is a return to the beginning. A time when we can take off the mask of seriousness and professionalism and return to being the child who dreams, laughs for no reason, and finds wonder in every little thing.

For many, work life is a whirlwind of commitments, responsibilities, and routines. We often lose touch with the part of us that yearns to live each moment with passion and curiosity. But now, without the pressures of work, is the perfect time to reconnect with those dreams and passions we have put aside.

Have you ever wondered what would have happened if you had pursued this career as a musician? Or if you had traveled more, explored faraway places and different cultures? Maybe you had a talent for painting or writing, but life took you down a different path. Well, now you have plenty of time and freedom to rediscover and cultivate those passions.

Start with small steps. Pick up that old journal you started years ago and finish it. Take an art class or learn to play a musical instrument. Travel to places you've always wanted to visit. Or, if you really want to go back in time, go to a playground and swing a little. It may sound silly, but I assure you that feeling the wind in your hair as you swing back and forth will take you back to a time when things were simpler.

Rediscovering your younger self does not necessarily mean doing everything we did when we were young. Rather, it means regaining that open-mindedness, that sense of wonder and curiosity that we had as children. It means looking at the world with new eyes and allowing ourselves to dream, explore, and experiment without fear.

And when you worry about what others will think, remember this: Retirement is the perfect time to be a little selfish. You have worked hard all your life, taken care of your family, and fulfilled your responsibilities. Now is the time to take care of yourself, rediscover who you really are, and live your life the way you want to.

In the end, you will discover that your true self, the child who was curious, passionate, and eager to explore the world, never really disappeared. It was just hidden under layers of responsibilities and expectations. And now, with the gift of retirement, you have the opportunity to bring it back into the light and embrace life with the same joy and wonder you once did.

Take a moment now to reflect on who you have been and who you want to be. Retirement offers a unique opportunity to go back and embrace that young self you miss so much. And when you do, you will find that life still has many adventures and surprises in store for you. Don't just live in nostalgia for the past; use those memories as a springboard to create new and exciting chapters in your life story.

Age? It's Just a Number You Lose Track Of

If we were to ask a child how old he is, he would probably proudly raise all his fingers, happy to announce his age to the world. But as we grow older, this initial excitement can turn into a quiet worry. We begin to perceive age as a series of limitations, an increasing number that mark our abilities and possibilities. In retirement, however, we can break free from these shackles and recognize a fundamental truth: age is just a number, and we often forget that.

Society, with its rigid definitions and expectations, has established that reaching a certain age means having certain abilities or limitations. But these are just conventions. How often have we heard stories of older people doing amazing things? The 60-year-old who runs his first marathon, the 80-year-old who learns to swim, the grandmother who decides to go skydiving on her 90th birthday. These are not exceptions, but examples of the human ability to overcome barriers, even those imposed by age.

The body changes over time, it is true, but that does not mean you have to accept a diminished version of yourself. The wisdom, experience, and skills gained over the years are invaluable resources that can and should be used. For every sign of physical wear and tear, there is a wealth of knowledge and insight that can be brought into play.

Perhaps instead of focusing on what we cannot do because of our age, we should focus on what we can do because of our age. At 20, we may have the energy to dance the night away, but at 60 or 70, we have the wisdom to appreciate moments, understand the nuances of life, and offer valuable advice based on decades of experience.

Retirement is an opportunity to free ourselves from social conventions and define our own path, regardless of age. It is not about denying the passage of time, but about embracing it and using it to your advantage. Age should not be seen as a limitation, but as an accumulation of years lived, experiences and wisdom.

It is also surprising how much attitude can affect physical perception. Those who see themselves as "old" tend to feel and act that way. On the other hand, those who see themselves as "young" bring a vitality and enthusiasm that positively influence their health and well-being.

Laughing, playing, dreaming-these are all activities that are ageless. We are the ones who choose to put them aside, but we can just as easily welcome them back into our lives. And if someone were to ask you how old you are, you might reply with a mischievous smile, "*I've stopped counting!*"

Even in the world of science, age is increasingly seen not as a determining factor, but as one element among many. Research suggests that mental attitude can have a significant impact on the aging process. A positive view of aging can actually lead to greater longevity and a better quality of life.

While the body may show signs of the passage of time, the mind remains eternal. Age, with all its numbers, cannot define who we really are, nor can it limit what we can do. Retirement offers a unique opportunity to rewrite one's story, to defy convention, and to live with passion, regardless of the numbers on the calendar. After all, if age were truly a definitive indicator of our abilities, history would be devoid of all the wonderful adventures experienced by those who dared to challenge that simple number. How about you, have you decided how you are going to live the next chapters of your life? If not now, when?

2. Eternal Springtime in the Mind

After navigating the meanders of deep reflection (and perhaps losing a few hairs in the process), we are now in a place where the sun always shines, at least in our minds. Don't get me wrong: I'm talking about our fabulous ability to stay fresh and young, not a tropical paradise (although, let's face it, that wouldn't be bad!). And while the idea of lying under a palm tree may sound appealing, I have an even more exciting suggestion: why not grow a palm tree in your mind?

Now, before you start looking for suggestions on how to grow trees in your mind (spoiler: not a good idea), let me explain. Retirement, my friend, is not only a time to relax and enjoy the joys of life, but also an opportunity to rekindle the enthusiasm and curiosity we had as children. You can think of your mind as a garden, and with the right care and attention, you can make it flourish in every season of life.

You may be wondering how. Well, I have an answer for you! (And no, it doesn't involve gardening tools or fancy fertilizers.) All you need is a dash of imagination, a handful of courage, and, of course, our trusty old sense of humor. Get ready to flood your inner garden with laughter, surprises, and who knows, maybe even some new hobbies or adventures.

And if you find yourself humming "in my secret garden" as you read these words, know that you are on the right track. Now grab your imaginary gardener's hat and follow me: it's time to explore this world of eternal mental springtime, where every day can be a new adventure! And remember, when your mind starts to feel the weight of the years, just sprinkle a little cheerfulness on it and you're done. Go on, there is so much to discover!

Passions So Hidden They Surprise Everyone

Oh, the passions! Those passions that, like a stubborn label on an old shirt, refuse to come off. But sometimes, let's face it, they are so well hidden that not even the most skilled detective could unearth them. But with retirement giving us time and freedom, we can finally go on the big treasure hunt to find those hidden gems.

Have you ever thought back to when you were a kid and wanted to be a paleontologist? Oh yes, those glorious days spent digging in the backyard, hoping to find a dinosaur bone, only to discover that you had unearthed the bones of Sunday dinner's chicken. Or maybe you've always had a passion for singing, but the only audience you've ever had is your shower. Well, now is the time to rediscover those dreams and turn them into reality.

The beauty of hidden passions is that they are unexpected. Imagine your granddaughter's surprise when she discovers that her grandfather can tango! Or the admiration of your neighbors when you show off your harp skills in the backyard. The sky is the limit, and maybe there is no limit!

But how does one begin this exploration?
1. **The imaginary time machine.** Go back to your childhood. What did you like to do? Make a list, no

matter how crazy or unlikely it seems now. Did you have a passion for building ships in bottles? Were you obsessed with drawing cartoon characters? This list is your golden ticket.

2. **Things you never did but always wanted to do.** Are there activities or hobbies you've always wanted to try, but never had the chance or courage? Maybe a Thai cooking class or scuba diving. Retirement could be the perfect time to dive (literally and figuratively) into new adventures.
3. **The art of observation.** Look around you. The world is full of inspiration. Maybe seeing kids playing soccer in the park makes you want to join a local team. Or maybe the smell of freshly baked bread inspires you to become a master baker.
4. **Classes and workshops.** So many places offer classes for adults on a variety of topics. Whether it's art, music, dance, or something else, there's a world of possibilities out there. And who knows? You might discover that you have a hidden talent for ceramics or theater.
5. **Technology as an ally.** In this digital world, you can also explore online. There are platforms that offer courses on just about anything. Take a look and see what catches your eye.

Now, a word of caution: when you start digging, be prepared to be surprised. You may discover passions you didn't even know you had. Maybe a hidden talent for flying trapeze or a love of haiku poetry.

And here's the fun part: once you identify these passions, dive in. Not only will they bring you joy and satisfaction, but they will also surprise those around you. Imagine the admiration (and perhaps a touch of jealousy) of your friends when they discover that you have taken up woodcarving or growing rare orchids.

Such hidden passions are like spices in a recipe: they may not always be obvious, but they add flavor and depth. And as any great chef knows, it is the unexpected mix of ingredients that creates the most memorable dish. So, my friend, grab your magnifying glass and start your treasure hunt. Who knows what unexpected delights await you? And remember, in life, as in cooking, a dash of surprise makes everything taste better!

From the Chair to the Classroom: Just Be Awake to Learn

How often have you thought that the chair is your throne and the remote is your scepter? Oh yes, the sweet melody of your couch calling you to sit in front of the television. But, my friend, the chair is not your only royal throne. And the remote control... well, it has its limits.

Before you start watching another show about why ducks migrate (although, let's face it, it's really interesting), pause for a moment. Not that there's anything wrong with watching educational programs about nature, but why not become a protagonist in an exciting adventure of knowledge yourself?

"*Ah,*" you're thinking, "*but I'm retired, my time for learning is over.*"
Let's start again: Have you ever wondered why, despite all the promises you made to yourself, you never learned to play the saxophone? Or why you never took that art history class you wanted to take after watching that documentary on the Sistine Chapel? Or maybe you've always wanted to understand how

bitcoin works, even though just thinking about it gives you a headache?

Classrooms are not just for the young. And between you and me, you don't even have to go into a physical classroom. Well, yes, thanks to the magic of technology and an internet connection (the same one that allows you to watch crazy cat videos on YouTube), you can learn just about anything from the comfort of your own home.

There are web-platforms like Coursera, Udemy, and Khan Academy that offer courses on just about anything that might interest a curious mind like yours. And we're not just talking about monotonous, boring classes. Many courses are interactive, with videos, quizzes, and forums where you can chat with other enthusiasts.

And if you think these platforms are hard to use, trust me, they're easier to navigate than that old VCR you had in the 1990s. Plus, many of these tutorials are free; you can find any tutorial on YouTube. Free, my friend. And who can resist free?

If digital is not for you, fear not. There are plenty of night schools, community colleges, and training centers in every city. And who says you have to stay in your own town? Maybe it's time to book that study abroad trip to France you've always wanted to take.

But if you think learning only means reading books or taking classes, think again. Have you ever thought about learning a martial art? Or joining a dance club? Or maybe try astral photography? Look, if my cousin's grandmother can become a black belt in karate, who are you to limit yourself?

Let me also tell you that learning is not just about acquiring new skills. It is also a way to socialize and make new friends. Think of all the new friends you might meet in that pottery class or that Transcendental Meditation class.

Always remember that the mind, like a good wine, improves with age. Just because you've stopped working doesn't mean you have to stop working on your personal growth. And the next time you sit in your chair, instead of turning on the television, why not turn on your curiosity? Then, when you have learned something new, you can always go back to that chair and watch the ducks migrate with a new perspective.

Neighborhood Tours Like Safaris

If I told you that there was an unexplored jungle between the skyscrapers, the townhouses, and the bar around the corner, what would you say? You'd probably raise an eyebrow and exclaim, "Well, that bar has a wide variety of liquor, but I don't know if I'd call it a jungle!"

But stop and think for a moment. How many times have you walked around your neighborhood looking without seeing? How many strange creatures, situations, and landscapes have you missed? You don't have to go on safari to Africa; every time you step outside your door, you start an adventure!

Imagine wearing an explorer's hat, sunglasses, and maybe even one of those old-fashioned binoculars that extend like a telescope. Are you ready? Then begin your urban safari.

1. The neighborhood wildlife. Cats basking on low walls, dogs proudly strolling with their owners (or maybe they are the owners), pigeons discussing the latest neighborhood news. Keep your eyes peeled and you might discover that the neighbor's cat is secretly flirting with the lady's cat across the street. An animal soap opera could be unfolding around every corner!

2. The urban flora. The plants growing between the cracks in the sidewalks, the manicured flower beds, the old tree in the park. Have you ever noticed that every tree has a story? Maybe a love story was born underneath it, or maybe it's the secret meeting place of a chess-playing old men's club.

3. Hidden cultures. That exotic grocery store you've always ignored may turn out to be a window to a faraway world. And that side street you've never taken? It could lead you to an entirely different neighborhood with new languages, foods, and music.

4. Secret architectures. You may think you know every building in your neighborhood. But have you ever really looked? Get up early one morning and watch the aurora light up the old facades, revealing details you never noticed before. And that strange house with the shutters always closed? Who knows what secrets it holds.

5. Humans, the strangest creatures of all. Ah, humans! An inexhaustible source of intrigue, stories, and surprises. The lady who always sings when she thinks she is alone, the boy with his strange collection of hats, the old man who tells stories of the "good old days" to anyone who will listen.

People-watching can be the best form of free entertainment, as long as you don't laugh too loudly and get their attention.

But as with any self-respecting safari, there are a few rules to follow:
- **Be respectful**. Don't stare too long or too hard, and don't trespass on private property, even if you think a rare "backyard lion" might be there.
- **Be curious, but discreet**. Ask questions, explore, but respect the privacy and boundaries of others.
- **Share your findings**. Maybe your neighbor didn't know he had a "rhino" (old statue) in his yard. Talk to your neighbors about it, and maybe you'll organize a group safari!

And if you are still skeptical about the magic of a neighborhood safari, try looking at it through a child's eyes. Children have this wonderful ability to see adventure everywhere, and with a little practice, maybe you can too.

So, the next time you think you need to travel to a faraway land for a new adventure, remember that adventure may be just around the corner, hidden in the streets of your neighborhood. Why look for lions in Africa when you can find cats, stories, and magic right here?

Board Games: When Monopoly Comes to Life

Board games! Those dusty boxes in the attic that hold worlds of adventure, strategy, and, if it's Monopoly, much, much frustration. But what if I told you that you could bring the excitement, betrayal, and alliances of board games into your real life, right into the heart of your neighborhood? Well, roll up your sleeves, because we're about to do just that.

1. Property and rentals. Let's start with Monopoly, the game that destroyed many friendships and families. Every time you walk through your neighborhood, think of every building, park, or landmark as property to buy. Each time you pass by, pay a mental "rent." It's a fun way to think of your neighborhood as a giant game board. And the good news is, in reality, there is no risk of going to jail!

2. Secret mission. Games like Risk have secret missions for players to complete. Create a "mission" for yourself every time you go out. It can be something as simple as "Find and greet three dogs" or something more complex like "Explore a place you've never been before." You'll be surprised at how much fun and challenge it can be.

3. Explore your Trivial Pursuit neighborhood. Taking a cue from Trivial Pursuit, why not create a quiz about your neighborhood? Ask questions about the history of the place, fun facts, or architectural details that may have escaped most people. Then, the next time you have guests, challenge them to a duel of neighborhood knowledge. They will surely gain a new respect for the place, and who knows, maybe even a little statuette to take home as a trophy!

4. The Goose Trail. In a re-enactment of the classic game of Goose, draw a "trail" through your neighborhood. Any point of interest can become a box. When you reach a "trap," perhaps an ice cream parlor or a coffee shop, you must stop and take a break. But beware! When you hit the "bridge," it may mean a long ride or a little de tour. One thing is for sure: you will never get bored.

5. Strategy challenges. Taking a cue from strategy games, try to figure out how to "defend" your neighborhood from a hypothetical invasion by... giant rabbits? Or maybe pizza-hungry zombies? Where would you deploy your "troops?"

What buildings would be strategic? It's a fun and imaginative way to see your neighborhood in a whole new light.

Now, before anyone calls me crazy, let me be clear: I'm obviously not suggesting that you turn your neighborhood into a giant board game with real pieces and giant dice (although, let's face it, that would be epic). The idea is to use your creativity and imagination to see the place you live in a new and fun way.

And don't forget the most important lesson of board games: the fun isn't in winning, it's in playing. So, as you explore your neighborhood with new eyes, remember to enjoy every moment, every discovery, every laugh. After all, it is not the destination that matters, but the journey. And what a journey it will be, through the winding streets, hidden alleys, and bustling plazas of your magical neighborhood!

3. Hobbies: Hidden Surprises in Everyday Life

Have you ever noticed how some retirees have that sparkle in their eyes? I'm not talking about the rust accumulated over the years, or the sparks from a shorted pacemaker. No, I'm talking about the bright light of someone who has made an amazing discovery: the surprise of being in the middle of everyday life, with all the time in the world and an endless list of hobbies at your fingertips.

Here, retirement is a kind of treasure hunt. Although, unlike pirates, you don't need a map or to dig holes in your backyard (although you could, if gardening is your hobby!). Hobbies are like the gold nuggets of everyday life. They're there, hidden under a veneer of "things I've always wanted to do," and now is the time to collect them!

Think of everyday life as a garage sale. Whereas before you were too busy running from one side to the other, now you have the luxury of wandering through the booths and finding hidden gems where you least expect them. Maybe starting with a seedling on the terrace and ending with a rock band in the garage, every day can be an adventure.

What if someone tells you that your new hobby seems a little... unusual? Answer with a smile like a true adventurer and remind them that someone once looked up at the sky and thought, "*I think I'll try flying!*" And voila, the airplane was born! Now, maybe your handmade sweater won't revolutionize the world like the airplane, but it will certainly keep someone warm during the winter. And isn't that a revolution in its own small way?

So, my friends in search of daily surprises, get ready to explore the wonders of hobbies hidden in the folds of your routine. And as the DIY experts say, "*It's never too late to start ... and make a little mess!*"

Terrace Gardening: The Sky Is the Limit

Have you ever stared at your balcony or terrace with the same feeling you get when you open the refrigerator, hoping for a culinary miracle, only to find stale cheese and onions? Ah, the disappointment! But now imagine transforming that terrace into a lush green oasis where the only limit is the sky. And maybe the neighbor's wall, but who cares?

Terrace gardening is like magic, and you are the wizard! Or the magician. It is an art that allows you to create your own little earthly paradise suspended in the clouds. Or at least on the third floor.

First, you don't need a green thumb to garden. Brown, blue or even neon pink will do. The key is passion and a dash of creativity. And maybe a dash of fertilizer.

Here are some ideas for turning your terrace into a garden:
- **Flower boxes, not just for flowers**. Sure, window boxes are the classic. But who says they have to be all flowers? There are aromatic plants like rosemary, mint and basil that are a feast for the senses. And, not to be overlooked, they can be used to add a touch of class to your dishes!

- **Vertical gardens**. When space is at a premium, think vertical! Use trellises or hanging structures to grow your favorite plants. And if you find yourself singing "*And I'm going up...up...up,*" you've probably taken the "sky's the limit" concept too literally.
- **Miniature ponds**. Imagine having a quiet, serene little body of water on your balcony, with aquatic plants and maybe a few small fish. An oasis of peace that allows you to relax while sipping your morning coffee - or your evening martini. No one is judging.
- **Succulents and cacti**. If, like me, every plant you touch seems to be headed for premature extinction, then succulents and cacti are your salvation. They require little water and care and are perfect for adding an exotic touch to your terrace.
- **Oases for insects and birds**. Add some plants that attract butterflies, bees, and other beneficial insects. Maybe even a small bird feeder. You'll see, it's like a nature reality show, but without the commercials!
- **Play with light**. Lighting can make all the difference. Add soft lights or lanterns to create a magical atmosphere on summer evenings. Or on winter nights, if you have a good blanket and warm wine!
- **Furniture and accessories**. A comfortable chair, a small table, maybe a small fountain. The right accessories can make your terrace not just a garden, but a real outdoor living room!

A word of caution. While it can be a euphoric experience to immerse yourself in terrace gardening, it's good to remember to respect condominium and safety rules. We wouldn't want your hanging paradise to become the cause of an epic feud with your downstairs neighbor.

But those little bureaucratic details aside, terrace gardening is a wonderful and rejuvenating hobby. A way to socialize, experiment and, why not, get some healthy exercise.

And remember, every time you plant a seed or a plant, you are creating life. You are shaping a little piece of the world that bears your imprint. And it doesn't matter if that piece of the world is on a balcony on the third or fifth floor in the middle of the city. As a wise man said, or maybe it was my old drunk uncle, "*Even a small garden can have a big heart.*" And with that I wish you good gardening and ... may the sky be your limit!

Sports: Where Experience Beats Young Legs

My friend, allow me to paint a scene for you: a gentleman in his later years, with a slightly distended belly, stands at the starting line of a race. To his right is a lean, muscular young man in shorts short enough to show most of his shaved legs. Yes, shaved. I guess that's the fashion these days.

The starting gun sounds and... Well, make no mistake, the young man takes off like a rocket, while our older hero walks with a gait that could be described as ... meditative. But don't underestimate the experience!

While the young run for victory, the old run for history. Experience teaches that it is not always about who gets there first, but who truly enjoys the journey. And in the world of sports, experience has its appeal, especially when it beats young legs.

Here are three sports where experience reigns supreme:

1. **Chess**. While some may not consider it a "sport" in the traditional sense, anyone who has ever faced a game of chess knows that it is a mental battle. It's not just about making quick moves, it's about anticipating your opponent's moves, developing a strategy, and sometimes making a good move.
2. **Bowls**. This is a sport where experience really shines! It is not about pure strength, but about judgment, calculation and sometimes a little reverse psychology. After all, how many bowls matches have been decided by careful measurement and a little negotiation about who is really closest to the ball?
3. **Golf**. Technique, patience, and course knowledge. Golf is not just about hitting the ball hard; it is about knowing how to aim it. And there is nothing like watching your young opponent's powerful swing send the ball into the lake while you make a calibrated move to place it close to the hole.

Other great sports for retirees:

- **Swimming.** Great for joints and endurance. You don't have to be Michael Phelps, just do a few laps regularly to maintain your fitness and well-being.
- **Walking**. It may sound simple, but a good walk, perhaps in the mountains or a nice park, can do wonders for your health and morale.
- **Table tennis**. Less challenging than traditional tennis, but just as much fun. And, as with bocce, strategy and experience count for a lot here.

- **Cycling**. You don't have to ride the Tour de France, but a nice ride in the country or around town will keep you active and allow you to discover new places.

Remember, it's not about competing like it's the Olympics, it's about enjoying the activity, making new friends and, of course, keeping your body and mind fit. And at the end of the day, when the youngsters are exhausted and ready for a nap, our retired hero may still have a few tricks up his sleeve - perhaps a good book or a nice glass of wine to end the day on a high note!

Creativity: From Quirky Sweaters to Artistic Selfies

My friend, when we talk about creativity in retirement, we are not talking about a simple pair of colorful socks or a tie with dancing parrots. Oh, no, we're venturing into territory where the only limit is your imagination (and maybe the occasional backache)!

Extravagant sweaters: The art of teasing

So, if you think fashion is the preserve of young and famous designers, I invite you to consider a category of clothing so bold and affirming that it would turn anyone's head: the extravagant sweater. Now we're going to dip our hands (and maybe a pair of needles) into the colorful, whimsical, and decidedly warming world of handmade sweaters. Imagine walking down the street and turning heads, not because you pulled the toilet paper roll off the sole of your shoe, but because your sweater screams audacity!

Liberated style. When you start designing a sweater, think of a young child with a palette of colors. He has no rules, no fears. If he wants a purple dinosaur with butterfly wings, he draws it! What about you? Do you want flying sheep on your sweater? Make them glide!

Materials. Choosing yarn is like choosing wine. There are light, fruity ones like mohair, and full-bodied, sturdy ones like cotton. And then there's polyester, which... well, it's like the Lambrusco of knitting.

Learning points. If the last time you picked up a knitting needle was while trying to unlock your car, fear not! There are community centers, YouTube tutorials, and, of course, grandmothers willing to impart wisdom and technique. They are like Hogwarts wizards, but with more cookies.

Variation. Try different techniques. Knit shaved, ribbed, braided. The world is full of possibilities, and your sweater can be more varied than an appetizer buffet.

Accessories. Who says a sweater only needs yarn? Add buttons, beads or, if you're feeling really daring, little bells. Walking and jingling are a new trend, I promise!

Challenge. If you're feeling adventurous, I challenge you to make a sweater for every holiday of the year. Yes, even International Chocolate Day. A cocoa-colored sweater with pockets full of chocolates, what do you think?

Scrapbooking: Paper memories in a digital world

As the world plunges into the digital age, where photos are lost in the abyss of cell phones and memories are stored on hard drives, there is still one nostalgic corner that refuses to go away: scrapbooking. My friend, isn't it ironic that in an age when we can send messages across continents in a fraction of a second, we still want to cut, paste, and embellish our memories by hand? But then again, who hasn't wanted to freeze and frame a special moment, not just with a click, but with their heart?

A dive into the past. Scrapbooking isn't just a hobby, it's a journey. Each page you turn takes you back, like a manual time machine, making you smile, maybe shed a tear, but always with a warm feeling.

Basic materials. You don't need the whole craft store. Some basic materials are card stock, scissors, glue, and of course those photos that are lying around in some drawer.

Tell a story. Each page in your scrapbook can tell a story. And no, I'm not just talking about that trip to Hawaii. Or the time the cat decided to jump in the laundry hamper. Or the movie ticket from that first date with the amazing chili popcorn.

Creative techniques. Experiment with techniques like embossing (to add texture to your pages) or "journaling" (adding little anecdotes or quotes next to your photos).

Classes and communities. If you're feeling a little lost, there are plenty of online and offline classes where scrapbooking enthusiasts gather to share techniques and often laugh about that terrible haircut, we all had in the 1980s.

Storage. Now that you've put hours and love into your book, be sure to store it away from direct light and moisture. You don't want your precious memories to become fodder for woodworms or fade like an old newspaper, do you?

In a world where speed and efficiency have become king and queen, take a moment to slow down. With scrapbooking, you're not just preserving memories, you're weaving a blanket of moments that have formed the fabric of your life. And as a certain gentleman with a sharp pen would say (er, that's me in a previous life), "*In the rush of life, sometimes it's nice to take a walk, especially with a beautiful scrapbook under your arm!*"

Sculpture: Creation in 3D

While some people are convinced that three dimensions are only for real life, true artists know that they can bring inert matter to life, transforming it into works that almost seem to breathe. Think about it: while many of us struggle to draw a straight line, there are a few brave souls who decide to go a step further and embrace the three-dimensional world. Sculpture has the magical power to transform a formless mass into something tangible and meaningful. It can represent emotions, tell stories, or simply decorate your space. And if someone objects that sculpture is an art that requires years of practice, just reply, "*But dear friend, don't the years sculpt us?*"

The basics of sculpting. While some people think you need a block of marble and a hammer, all you really need to get started is a desire to create and, well, something to sculpt.

Beginner materials. Clay, plasticine, or even good old Play-Doh. They are inexpensive, easy to shape, and perfect for getting started. And remember, if your first attempt looks more like a shapeless blob than a masterpiece, you can always start over.

Essential tools. While your hands are the main tools, you may want a few accessories. Small chisels, trowels, rollers, and for the more ambitious, a small pottery wheel.

Basic techniques. Don't be too hard on yourself at first. Start with simple shapes, such as spheres or cubes, and slowly add detail. Before you know it, you may have a small army of creatures on your table.

Classes and workshops. If you are feeling a little lost or just want some inspiration, look for workshops or classes in your area. The beauty of sculpting is that you can learn a lot by watching others.

Safety first. Remember that you are working with tools that can be sharpened. Let your enthusiasm guide you, but always use caution. There is no need to become a work of art yourself!

Artistic selfie: Who said only the young can dominate Instagram?

Ah, the selfie! This art form is as old as... well, let's say the invention of camera phones. Once upon a time, a self-portrait required hours of posing in front of a painter, at the risk of being portrayed as Frankenstein's third cousin. Now, thanks to the magic of technology, we can portray ourselves as real Adonis or Aphrodite -- or at least make the most of what Mother Nature has given us. But wait a minute! Who said selfies were only for the younger generation? Well, maybe that grandson who's trying to tell you how Instagram works for the tenth time, but don't listen to him! There's a whole world of artistic selfies out there, and with a little creativity and the right angle, anyone can shine.

Here's how to take your "selfie" from ordinary to extraordinary:

- **The perfect angle**. The beauty of a selfie is all in the angle. Who needs to see that little double chin when you can tilt your phone slightly and give the impression of a jawline carved by Michelangelo?

- **Filters, but in moderation**. Filters are like salt; a little can enhance the flavor, too much can ruin the dish. A filter can add warmth or a vintage effect to your shot, but don't overdo it. You don't want to look like Andy Warhol's Pop Art.
- **Scenery and backgrounds.** Are you in the garden? Position yourself next to a blooming rose. Are you in a museum? Take a selfie with that statue as if it were your best friend. Context can take your selfie from something ordinary to a work of art.
- **Accessories and poses**. A chic hat, a pair of trendy sunglasses, or a colorful scarf can add that extra touch. And when it comes to poses, remember that there are no rules. Want to give a wink or a thumbs up like an enthusiastic tourist? Go for it!
- **Interaction and story**. There's nothing like a selfie to tell a story. Whether you're celebrating your 50th anniversary or just baked a cake, let the world know what you're doing and why it's special.
- **Advanced editing apps**. In an age where every phone has its own little editing suite, why not take it to the next level? Download apps like Snapseed, Lightroom Mobile, or VSCO. These apps are the best-kept secrets of those who publish stunning photos. You can fix imperfections, play with color saturation, or even turn an ordinary photo into a masterpiece worthy of an art gallery.
- **Appropriate hashtags.** While you might be tempted to use #wildguy or #crazynight, you might want to opt for something more appropriate like #smartandsexy or #iwillneverbetoooldforthis.

Remember, there is no age limit when it comes to expressing yourself, and a selfie is worth a thousand words. So, the next time you're out and about and feeling particularly radiant, pull out your phone, snap a picture and share it with the world. And if someone tells you you're too old for Instagram, just reply, *"I'm too young in spirit to limit myself!"* And then, who knows, you might become an influencer for the silver generation.

Rock Stars in the Church Choir

Have you ever walked by a church and heard a song that made you think you were at a concert by a famous rock band? Well, it could be that your local rock star has infiltrated the church choir.

The transformation from pew to stage

You wake up one Sunday morning, and as you sip your coffee, it hits you like a bolt of lightning: you want to sing! Not in the shower, no. You want everyone to hear your voice. And what better place to start than your local church? You're ready to unleash your hidden talent, and the church choir is waiting for you with open arms.

Ah, how I remember the first time! I arrived thinking I was going to be an extra, and instead I ended up in the spotlight. During one of the rehearsals, a particularly inspired "Ave Maria" earned me a smile and a pat on the back. But the real triumph was seeing Grandma across the street waving her fan like she was at a rock concert. Who would have thought? From pulpit to rock star, the step was short and incredibly melodious. That's the beauty of life: surprises and applause can happen where you least expect them.

Benefits of being a church rock star:
1. **New friends and admirers**. And who would have thought? Mrs. Rosina, in the little wool hat, has a vibrato that would make Pavarotti jealous.

2. **Sparkly dresses**. Forget the boring gray dress; you can customize your choir robe with sequins and glitter.
3. **Let me hear that beat**. Singing improves memory, mood, and, some say, even helps tone your tummy. (But I can't vouch for a flat stomach!)
4. **Guaranteed sold-out shows**. The church is packed every Sunday. Okay, maybe they came for other reasons, but you can guess the main reason.

A journey from bass to soprano:

- **The bass**. Roars like a lion, but with more harmony. A deep sound that resonates in the soul.
- **The baritone**. The bass's big brother, with a touch of drama.
- **The Tenor**. The angelic voice that reaches high notes and makes some grandmas in the front row swoon.
- **The Soprano**. The pinnacle of perfection that can break a glass, or at least old beliefs.

But how does one become a choral legend? Here are some suggestions:

- **Warm up**. Vocal cords are like rubber bands; if you don't stretch them first, they can snap - figuratively speaking, I hope!
- **Drink water**. Keep your throat hydrated. A glass of wine may be tempting, but water is your best friend.
- **Listen and learn**. You can't always be the star. Listen to others, appreciate their talents, and steal a few tricks.
- **Don't be afraid to make mistakes**. If you miss a note, do it with style. After all, Elvis made a career out of a pelvic thrust, not note perfection!

And remember, every great artist started somewhere. Maybe Beyoncé started in the church choir, who knows? So put on that robe, straighten your back, and sing like it's the last time. And who knows, maybe the next time people walk by the church, they'll stop and listen to the rock star in you!

Of course, becoming a rock star in the church choir won't get you to the Grammy Awards, but it will definitely give you a sense of accomplishment, new friendships, and who knows, maybe even a secret fan club across the country. And if it all goes wrong, at least you tried and made the parishioners happy for a few Sundays!

Backyard Astrology: Easier Than Astronomy

In the vast and complex universe of retirement activities, backyard astrology has always had a place of honor next to growing giant tomatoes and trying to understand the instructions on new electronic devices. Now, if you are like me, you might think that astrology and astronomy are the same thing. Well, you'd be wrong. Astronomy involves telescopes, complicated formulas, and sleepless nights staring at the stars. Astrology, on the other hand, requires only a little imagination, a newspaper, and a belief that Mercury retrograde is the cause of all your problems.

A backyard, a horoscope, and... you!

Have you ever looked up at the stars and wondered, "*What the hell are they trying to tell me?*" Here, with backyard astrology, you can finally get some answers, though maybe not the ones you expect.

Your Backyard Astrologer Kit
1. **A comfortable chair.** Astrology requires patience. And by patience, I mean the time you spend sitting and thinking about why your sign didn't win the lottery.
2. **A newspaper or magazine.** These are essential. Not to read the news, but to consult the horoscope. Yes, modern astrology is based on very old sources: the horoscope section of your favorite magazine.
3. **A star chart.** Useful if you want to look like you know what you're doing.
4. **A pen and notebook.** To write down all the wrong predictions and laugh about them the next year.

Decipher the stars, or at least try to:
- **The Sun**: It represents your ego. Even if you can't look at it directly, it knows you're there, and it worships it, hoping it will tell you something useful.
- **The Moon**: Your emotionality. That's why you cry every time you see a tear-jerker movie or drop your ice cream on the floor.
- **Mercury**: Communication. When it's in retrograde, it's like the signal on your cell phone goes out. Everything becomes chaos!

The signs of the zodiac - a quick and dirty guide

Aries. Impulsive, always in motion. The backyard Aries might decide to plant a tree in the middle of the lawn just because it seemed like a good idea at the time.

Taurus. Stubborn and comfortable. Refuses to change his lawn chair even though it is 20 years old and creaking.

Gemini. Dual personality. Decides to worship astrology one day and astronomy the next.

Cancer. Sentimental and domestic. Would build a small planetarium in their backyard just to hear the stars closer.

Leo. Born to shine. Doesn't need a telescope to see the stars - they're already the star of their own backyard!

Virgo. Perfectionist and meticulous. Has a special book in which he notes every time the horoscope is wrong.

Libra. Always looking for balance. Doesn't know whether to believe the newspaper horoscope or his astrology app. So he reads both.

Scorpio. Intense and mysterious. Says he doesn't believe in astrology but knows exactly when Mercury is retrograde.

Sagittarius. Adventurous and optimistic. Only reads the horoscope for travel and adventure predictions, even if it's just walking around the yard.

Capricorn. Practical and ambitious. Doesn't have time for horoscopes, but if they tell him it's going to be a good day for business, he won't say no.

Aquarius. Innovative and a bit eccentric. Trying to invent a new way of reading the stars, perhaps using only mismatched socks.

Pisces. Dreamer and intuitive. Although the chart says otherwise, he believes that every day is perfect for daydreaming.

With backyard astrology, you won't become the next Nostradamus or accurately predict the future. But you'll have a great reason to sit under the stars, reflect on life, and, who knows, find a new perspective-or at least a good laugh at how funny your horoscope reading is.
So, arm yourself with a star chart, a newspaper, and a good sense of humor, and go look at the stars. They may not tell you your future, but they will certainly light up your night!

4. Places That Google Maps Is Still Looking For

The world is a big, mysterious place! And you, my friend, may think you've seen it all thanks to that cute little blue pointer app on your phone, but I can assure you that there are places even the almighty Google Maps hasn't seen yet. And no, I'm not talking about Narnia, although it would be fascinating to come face-to-face with a talking lion after passing a wardrobe.

But imagine finding a little hidden corner, a place that has never seen the shadow of a tourist with a camera around his neck, or a barista asking if you want Wi-Fi before he even serves you your coffee. Yes, these places still exist, and believe me, they are the panacea for every retiree's adventurous soul.

You may ask, "*But where are these magical places?*" Well, they are the hidden gems, the places off the beaten path, the places where chickens cross the road for no reason and time seems to stand still.

Be forewarned, though: finding these places requires a bit of a pioneering spirit and maybe an old, yellowed map you might find in the attic. But the reward? Besides the satisfaction of saying, "*Here's a place Google Maps doesn't know about,*" you get to have authentic experiences away from the hustle and bustle of modern life.

So, let's start this journey by exploring some of these wonderful hidden corners of the world. And don't worry, I've thought of everything, even some practical details to make the adventure a little less... adventurous. Fasten your seatbelts, or rather your hiking boots, and get ready for endless discovery!

Off the Beaten Path Destinations

Have you ever noticed how certain places are crowded with tourists, while others remain hidden, like treasures waiting to be discovered? Why does everyone know about the Eiffel Tower, but few know about the enchanted villages hidden in the Alps? Here, your retirement is the perfect passport to explore these unknown corners, far from the masses, but close to the true essence of the places.

The advantage of age? You can say that you've been to places that the young man at the bar next to you doesn't even know exist!

European villages where nature steals the show:
- **Hallstatt, Austria**. If fairies existed, this is where they would live. Pastel-colored houses, snow-capped mountains, and a fairy-tale lake.
- **Gimmelwald, Switzerland**. Ever dreamed of living in a Milka chocolate landscape? This is the place for you!
- **Matera, Italy**. City of caves and cave churches, a dive into prehistory with all the modern conveniences.

Asian paradises right out of the catalog:
- **Luang Prabang, Laos.** Monks, temples, and night markets. Yes, you read that right, night markets! Who needs sleep when you have so much to explore?
- **Bhutan**. You pay a small fortune to get in, but you end up in a country where happiness is officially measured. Price. Priceless.

America's hidden jewels:
- **Skagway, Alaska**. The Last Frontier. Bears, mountains, and the feeling of being a prospector. I can't guarantee gold, but memories are treasures!
- **Valle de Guadalupe, Mexico**. Did you say wine? This little Napa Valley will give you an ethyl tour of vineyards and chapels.

Get lost in the wonders of Africa:
- **Lamu, Kenya**. Away from the crowded safaris, Lamu is an island forgotten by time. Sand roads, donkeys as the main means of transportation and a blend of Arab, African, and Persian cultures.
- **Chefchaouen, Morocco**. The blue city hidden between the Rif mountains. A feast for the eyes and for photographers. But don't tell too many people!

Oceania's hidden gems:
- **Lord Howe Island, Australia**. Restricted to a few visitors at a time, this is a nature lover's paradise. Snorkel with stingrays and turtles in crystal clear waters. And the best part? No crowds!
- **Stewart Island, New Zealand.** The only thing next to this island is Antarctica. A perfect place to see the southern lights and stars like never before.

The unexpected charms of the Middle East:
- **Salalah, Oman**. During the monsoon season, the hills turn emerald green. A small oasis far from modern metropolises, with incense-scented markets.
- **Byblos, Lebanon**. One of the world's oldest cities, where the alphabet is said to have been born. Beaches, ruins and a vibrant nightlife.

Some practical tips:
- **Socialize**. When visiting these hidden places, talk to the locals. They are a goldmine of stories and anecdotes.
- **Avoid high season**. Yes, you may have to deal with some rain or less-than-perfect weather, but you'll have the streets to yourself!
- **Document yourself**. Before you go, pick up a few books or articles about the area. Not the usual guidebooks, but ones written with passion by people who have actually lived there.
- **Stay safe**. Yes, you're an adventurer, but don't forget to check out the safety conditions of the place. And of course, a good travel insurance policy never hurts!
- **Eat local**. Forget the fast-food chains and dive into the stalls, markets, and taverns. You might discover your new favorite dish - or at least a funny story to tell the grandchildren!

And always remember, O intrepid explorer, that the goal is not the destination, but the journey itself. Every unexplored corner, every dirt road, every laugh with a new friend is a page in the best chapter of your life.

A wise man once said, *"The world is a book, and those who do not travel read only one page."*

How many pages do you want to read?

Italy: Postcard Villages Without Postcards

Italy, ah, dear old, lovely Italy! The land of pizza, pasta, and love at first sight. And while Rome, Florence and Venice are often the first stops for lovers of the bel paese, it was the small villages that stole my heart. Yes, me, who spent weeks exploring these tiny hidden gems. By the way, if you find a wide-brimmed hat and an old camera nearby, it might be mine. I tend to forget things when I am open-mouthed at the sights.

Castelluccio, Umbria

Why go: For the flowers! Every summer, the plains of Castelluccio are transformed into a carpet of poppies, gentians, and daisies.

What to do: Enjoy a walk through the flowering fields and taste Castelluccio's famous lentils.

A little secret: The village offers incredible views of the Sibillini Mountains. Ideal for a picnic in the mountains!

Alberobello, Puglia

Why go: Trulli, trulli and more trulli! These distinctive cone-shaped buildings are unique in the world.

What to do: Stroll the cobblestone streets, visit a trulli church and stay in one of these distinctive buildings.

A little secret: Avoid high season. In spring or fall, you'll have the country almost to yourself!

Bormida, Liguria

Why go: It's one of those places that seemed destined for oblivion until the mayor suggested paying people to move there. A brilliant initiative!

What to do: Stroll through its deserted streets and enjoy the tranquility of a place out of time.

A Little secret: The local food is delicious. Try the pesto!

Civita di Bagnoregio, Lazio

Why go: Dubbed "the dying town" because of erosion, Civita is a jewel perched on a hill.

What to do: Explore the cobblestone streets, take in the views of the valley, and refresh your spirit in this magical place.

A little secret: Visit at night when there are few tourists and the lights of the sunset make it shine.

Santo Stefano di Sessanio, Abruzzo

Why go: A perfectly preserved medieval village 1250 meters above sea level, surrounded by the majestic Gran Sasso mountains.

What to do: Explore the village, visit the medieval tower, and if you're feeling adventurous, go horseback riding nearby.

A little secret: The village is famous for its lentils. Be sure to try them, perhaps in a tasty soup!

Vernazza, Liguria

Why go: One of the five villages in the Cinque Terre, Vernazza is an enchantment of bright colors overlooking the sea.

What to do: Enjoy a fresh gelato while sitting on the pier, admiring the sea and colorful buildings.

A Little secret: Don't forget to visit the church of Santa Margherita d'Antiochia, a small architectural jewel.

Castelmezzano, Basilicata

Why go: One of the most beautiful villages in Italy, nestled in the Lucanian Dolomites.

What to do: Are you an adrenaline junkie? Try the Flight of the Angel, a zip line through the mountains.

A Little secret: If you can get up early, the sunrise here is simply magical.

My friend, I want to tell you one very important thing: Don't trust the GPS! In one village it led me to a "bridge". It turned out to be a ford. The result? Wet pants and an unforgettable experience.

Italy is much more than what you see on postcards or TV. Each village is a universe in itself, full of stories, flavors, and smiles. And if you are in one of these places and see a guy looking lost, stop and offer him a coffee. That could be me, still looking for my hat!

In Search of Coffee... Anytime, Anyhow!

Once upon a time there was a man in search of the elixir of long life. No, I am not talking about a magic potion, but about Neapolitan coffee with its legendary cremina. My friend, retirement has its advantages, and one of them is the time you can devote to your passions, and what passion can be greater than a nice cup of coffee made to perfection?

One sunny morning, while strolling through the alleys of Naples, the sound of coffee machines sizzling like the wings of a thousand cicadas led me to the city's best-kept secret: cremina. Oh, it's not just any cream, it's the liquid gold that crowns any coffee worthy of the name!

Here is how it is made, according to the old priests of Neapolitan coffee:
1. **The first sacrifice**. As soon as the coffee comes out, you must catch its first drops. These creamy, intensely flavored drops are like the soul of the coffee. Put them in a bowl with the sugar.
2. **The sacred dance**. While the coffee continues its ritual, you must perform yours. With circular movements, almost like a dance, mix the sugar and coffee with a teaspoon. The intensity with which you perform this step will determine the majesty of the cremina. So, my friend, mix with all your heart!

3. **The last magic.** Now, with a generous gesture, pour a teaspoon of cremina into each cup as if to bless it. Then pour the coffee with respect and admiration.

As I followed these steps, I felt the warmth of tradition and passion enveloping each cup of coffee. It reminded me how much each day of retirement could be enriched by a small ritual, a moment of sharing, or an unexpected discovery.

And so, every time I make my coffee, I think back to that morning in Naples, its alleys, its smiles, and the magic that can come from a simple cup of coffee. As they say in Naples, "'*O cafè 'e 'na vota, nun se scorda maje!*" (The coffee of the past, you never forget!).

The World in a Box: Geocaching

Ah, the eternal thirst for adventure! Some seek excitement through books, others through epic journeys to distant lands. And then there are those, like me, who prefer to stick their noses into little hidden boxes, hoping not to run into a spider or, worse yet, your ten-year-old grandmother's candy. I am, of course, talking about geocaching.

What in the world is geocaching? Well, imagine a treasure hunt on a global scale, where the whole world is your playground and you... well, you're there with a GPS in your hand and a fierce determination. And let me be clear, geocaching is not so much about the glory or the treasure as it is about the sheer fun of discovery.
Because, let's face it, you're never going to find a chest full of gold.

Quick guide to Geocaching:
1. **Start the GPS.** In the age of technology, forget the compass and old maps. Today, all you need is a GPS unit or simply a smartphone with GPS. And thank goodness, you don't have to worry about being attacked by pirates unless you're looking for a cache near a children's playground.
2. **Visit a geocaching website.** There are several sites, but "Geocaching.com" is the benchmark.
3. **Find a cache near you.** Once registered, enter your coordinates and you will be presented with a list of caches near you. Choose one, write down the coordinates and start your search.
4. **Go to the location and look for the cache.** It can be a small box, a pipe, or any other object that holds a log or small object.
5. **Sign the log.** Every cache has a log. Write your name, date, and any other message you want to leave for the next adventurer.
6. **Put the cache back exactly where you found it**. It's a game of honesty and respect for other players.

Now, you may be wondering what's in these little boxes. Oh, you can find anything from an old beer cap to a photo of a cat named Mr. Whiskers (true story). But it's often the simple act of searching and finding that gives you the satisfaction.

And if you have the urge to hide something, you can always create your own cache. Just follow the rules, such as not leaving food or dangerous items behind. Remember, the goal is not to make it impossible for others to find the cache, but rather to provide a fun challenge.

During my geocaching adventures, I have been lucky enough to meet other players. And I can tell you that there is no one type of geocacher. You might meet an old man with a walking stick or an excited kid in an adventurer's hat, both with the same bright light in their eyes.

Geocaching is not just about the hunt. It's about connecting with the world, nature, and people. And, if you will allow me a moment of seriousness, in an increasingly digitalized world, there is nothing better than unplugging, getting out and looking for something tangible.

If you have a sense of adventure, a GPS smartphone, and a few hours to spare, I suggest you give geocaching a try - it could be your next great passion. And who knows, maybe one day you'll stumble upon one of my hidden boxes. Happy hunting!

Themed Journeys: From Sherlock Holmes to Mummies

My friend, if you have ever watched a movie, read a novel, or watched a TV series and thought, *"I wish I could have an adventure like that,"* then you have come to the right place. Themed travel is the antidote to boredom, the salt of life, the secret ingredient that turns an ordinary trip into a legendary odyssey.

Sherlock Holmes: Between fog and mystery
   Where? Baker Street, of course! You are in the heart of London, shrouded in fog and mystery.
   What to do? Visit the Sherlock Holmes Museum. And maybe wear a wide-brimmed hat and a magnifying glass for that extra touch.

Tip: In the evening, try one of the city's themed escape rooms.

Vampires and castles: In search of Dracula

Where? Transylvania, Romania.

What to do? Visit Bran Castle, the (alleged) home of Dracula. And no, there are no actual vampires.

Tip: Bring garlic, sunglasses, and a sense of humor. Oh, and don't worry about the dark circles, they look great!

Hobbits and Middle-earth: In search of the ring

Where? New Zealand, actual Middle-earth.

What to do? Visit the filming locations for The Lord of the Rings and The Hobbit, including Hobbiton, the miniature Shire.

Tip: Remember to bring a map (and maybe a ring). And if you meet Gollum along the way, don't make him any promises you can't keep!

Samurai warriors and straw castles: Journey to the heart of feudal Japan

Where? Kyoto, Japan.

What to do? Explore ancient temples, Zen gardens and fortified castles while immersing yourself in samurai history.

Tip: If you can book an experience at a ryokan (a traditional Japanese hotel), you might even get to sleep on tatami mats and eat fresh sushi for breakfast!

Pirates and hidden treasures: In the footsteps of Jack Sparrow

Where? The Caribbean, paradise islands of adventure.

What to do? Visit ancient ruins of pirate forts, hunt for treasure (metaphorically speaking, of course), and sip rum under palm trees.

Tip: Don't forget your pirate hat and eye patch. And if anyone asks, *"Where did you park your ship?"* remember to answer with a hoarse *"Arrrrrr!"*

Mummies and Pyramids: Journey through time

Where? Egypt, land of the pharaohs.

What to do? Explore the Pyramids of Giza, the Egyptian Museum in Cairo, and, if you're feeling adventurous, take a cruise on the Nile.

Tip: If you do decide to search for the Pharaoh's lost treasure, remember to watch out for curses! But I bet a smart retiree like you will have no problem.

And a little bonus because I sense you have an adventurous soul.

Jedi Knights and distant stars: In a galaxy....

Where? Tunisia, where some iconic "Star Wars" scenes were filmed.

What to do? Explore abandoned movie sets in the desert and feel like you're on Tatooine.

Tip: Avoid mixing with the Tuskens and don't complain about the heat. It is the desert!

Now, my friend, put on your most comfortable shoes and venture out into the world!

Backpacking: A Borderless Retirement

There you have it, the art of backpacking! A method that many think is exclusive to young misers or philosophers and. But if you think so too, you are wrong, my friend. Because there is no age to become a backpacker, and if you don't believe me, just ask my old backpacker, veteran of countless adventures.

Why Backpacking? Let's take a look at the benefits:
- **Economy**. Maybe you have a decent pension, maybe you don't. Either way, why spend a fortune when you can travel cheap?
- **Minimalism**. What do you really need in your life? With a backpack, you will learn the art of living with the bare minimum. And no, you don't have to carry that bronze dachshund statue you bought in Vienna.
- **Freedom**. No suitcases to lug around, no strict check-in hours. You are free as air!

Now, to the uninitiated, backpacking might seem like a daunting task. But, as always, I'm here to guide you!

Before you go:
1. **Choosing a Backpack**. Don't buy the first backpack you see. Look for something ergonomic, with multiple pockets and adjustable straps. And no, that beach bag will not do.
2. **Contents**. The secret is essentials. A week's worth of clothes (you'll be able to wash them), a first aid kit, toiletries, and maybe that book you've always wanted to read but never found the time. Oh, and always bring an extra pair of socks, trust me.
3. **Budget**. Even if you're saving money, it's important to set a budget. How much can you afford to spend each day? Remember to include accommodations, food, transportation and, of course, souvenirs.

During the trip:
- **Lodging**. Hostels, B&Bs, guesthouses and, why not, platforms like Airbnb. Be open to sleeping in unusual places; you might end up in a tree house or an old castle.

- **Transportation**. Buses, trains, and hitchhiking (yes, even at a certain age). These are all valid ways to get around. And don't forget your legs, which, despite a few aches and pains, are perfect for walking and exploring.
- **Food**. Eat where the locals eat. Not only will you save money, but you'll get an authentic taste of the culture. What if you come across a dish, you don't even know the name of? That's part of the adventure!
- **Culture**. Unlike traditional tourists, you have time. Visit local markets, watch street performances, attend traditional festivals. And if someone invites you to a family dinner, don't say no!

On the way back:
1. **Stories to tell**. You will be the hero of every dinner party, the topic of every conversation. And when your grandson tells you about the time he went backpacking in Spain, you can reply, "*Ah, my boy, I beat you by 40 years!*"
2. **New friendships**. You'll meet people from all over the world. And don't worry about language; a smile and a few gestures are universal.
3. **Reflections**. Travel changes you. And I'm not just talking about the tan or the impulse tattoo. I'm talking about inner growth, about discovering sides of yourself you didn't even know you had.

My friend, adventurous retiree, if you still think backpacking is only for the young, think again. Life is a journey, and as they say, it's not the destination that matters, it's the journey itself. So, grab your backpack, fill it with the essentials, and hit the road. The world awaits you, and you have a guesthouse to explore!

5. Dishes, Glasses, and Occasional Messes

Who said retirement was the time to go on a diet? Well, probably the same person who suggested replacing good old wine with fennel herbal tea. Pff! Wine may not help you see clearly enough to read the newspaper, but I assure you, my friend, it will help you see life with brighter eyes!

Entering the kitchen as a retiree is like entering a playground without a janitor. Yes, there will be the occasional mess - perhaps a charred pizza or dough so stuck together you could use it as putty. But oh, the laughs you'll get making these homemade bombs! And if you can't laugh at your culinary messes, they'll at least give you a great story to tell your grandchildren or neighbors. *"Remember that time I tried to make a souffle and it turned into a crepe?"* Now that is what I call home entertainment!

But cooking is not just about cakes. It is also a journey through tastes, aromas, and memories. A pot of simmering ragu can take you back to the days when your grandmother spoiled you with her cooking. Or that exotic recipe you've always wanted to try? Now is the time. Retirement gives you the freedom to explore, experiment, and... eat.

And if you don't feel like cooking? Well, there are always the glasses. Whether it's fine wine, sparkling beer or spiced tea, each sip is a journey, a moment to celebrate. After all, living life to the fullest in retirement is all about taste!

It's time to immerse yourself in a world of flavor, adventure and... well, the occasional mess.

Flavors From Around the World... And From Your Home Bakery

Ever been to Bangkok? Or Marrakech? Or the corner of your kitchen where you keep forgotten spices and exotic flours? Well, in retirement, you have the opportunity to explore all these places...starting right here in your kitchen!

Start with a little trip. Imagine opening the spice drawer. Ah, the smell of curry that takes you back to the chaotic streets of Mumbai, or cinnamon that reminds you of an Istanbul bazaar. But what to do with these aromas that evoke distant landscapes? Well, the answer, my friend, is to cook!

Now, if you're thinking, *"But I can't even boil an egg,"* I say, *"All right!"* Retirement, among its myriad virtues, provides time, and time allows you to make messes, learn from your mistakes, and make new, bigger messes. The important thing is to have fun!

Remember the time you tried to make risotto and ended up with a kind of rice soup? That was a "liquid" version of the dish. Or the time you tried to make a cake and accidentally made a pancake? Call that a "culinary reinterpretation." Either way, you're creating something new, you're experimenting, and there's nothing more fun than that.

But let's not forget the home oven. That magical appliance that has the power to transform simple ingredients into delicious treats. Whether it's crispbread, roast chicken or, if you're feeling brave, an attempt at croissants (and who cares if they look more like doughnuts!), the home oven is your ticket to a gastronomic journey.

And for those who want more international flavors without the airfare, why not try dishes from faraway lands? Homemade sushi may seem intimidating, but I assure you, with a little practice and a lot of sticky rice, you'll feel like a real Japanese sushi chef-at least until you try using chopsticks!

Or, if you're like me, you might prefer some nice Italian pasta. And let me give you a little advice: while olive oil, garlic and tomato are the holy triad of Italian cuisine, the key is... love. Yes, yes, I know that sounds a little sweet, but I challenge you to make a sauce without a dash of love and see how it turns out.

And let's not forget desserts! Ah, the sweet world of desserts. From Italian tiramisu to French crème brûlée to Greek baklava. Every nation has its sin of gluttony, and in retirement you have the time and freedom to explore each one.

I know it is wonderful to travel and taste the typical dishes of each place, and I invite you to do so. But I want to tell you that if you want, you can travel the world from the comfort of your own home. All you need is a pinch of curiosity, a handful of ingredients, and a good sense of humor. And the best part? You don't have to worry about luggage, plane delays, or jet lag. Just enjoy!

Recipes With Anecdotes and Oil Stains

All the best recipes have a story behind them, and often an oil stain on the page to prove it. That, my friend, is proof that a recipe has been loved, tried, and... well, sometimes even a little fought over.

Here are 3 recipes from around the world:

Spaghetti Carbonara (Italy)

Ingredients:
- 15oz spaghetti
- 6oz guanciale (pork cheek)
- 4 egg yolks
- grated Pecorino Romano cheese
- black pepper
- a pinch of salt

Directions:
1. Bring water to a boil in a saucepan. Add salt.
2. Meanwhile, dice the guanciale and fry in a pan without oil until crisp.
3. In a bowl, beat the egg yolks with the grated pecorino cheese and black pepper until creamy.
4. Cook the spaghetti al dente, drain and add to the pan with the guanciale. Stir well.
5. Add the egg and cheese mixture, stirring quickly to prevent the egg from overcooking.
6. Serve immediately.

Anecdote: The name "carbonara" comes from the term "carbonaro" or charcoal burner. It is said that this pasta was a typical dish of the miners who worked in the mountains of Lazio. Another, perhaps more legendary, story suggests that the dish originated as a kind of "fast food" for American soldiers during World War II, combining eggs, bacon, and pasta.

Chicken Tikka Masala (India)

Ingredients:
- 4 chicken breasts, diced
- 2 tablespoons oil
- 1 chopped onion
- 3 cloves of garlic, chopped
- 1 tablespoon freshly grated ginger
- 2 tablespoons tomato sauce
- 1 package of cooking cream
- spices: turmeric, coriander, cumin, paprika, garam masala
- salt to taste

Directions:
1. In a large saucepan, heat the oil and sauté the onion, garlic, and ginger.
2. Add the tomato sauce and spices, stirring for a few minutes.
3. Add the chicken and cook until golden brown.
4. Add the cream and simmer for about 20 minutes or until the chicken is cooked through and the sauce has thickened.
5. Serve with basmati rice or naan bread.

Anecdote: Although considered a classic of Indian cuisine, chicken tikka masala has British origins. Legend has it that a customer asked for a sauce for his dry chicken tikka and the chef added a can of tomato sauce and cream, resulting in this dish.

Chocolate Churros (Spain)

Ingredients:
- 1 glass of water
- 2oz butter
- 1 pinch of salt
- 5oz flour
- oil for frying
- sugar
- 3oz dark chocolate
- 1 glass of whipping cream

Directions:
1. Bring the water, butter, and salt to a boil in a saucepan.
2. Remove from heat and add flour, stirring until smooth.
3. Pour the mixture into a star tip pastry bag.
4. Heat the oil in a frying pan and when it is hot, add the dough sticks and fry until golden brown.
5. Remove from heat and sprinkle with sugar.
6. For the chocolate cream: melt the chocolate in a double boiler and add the cream, stirring until smooth.
7. Serve the churros hot with the chocolate cream.

Anecdote: Although popular in Spain, churros are said to have been invented by shepherds in the mountains, where they were easier to make and cook over an open fire.

While these recipes are delicious as is, I encourage you to add your own personal touch. And if you happen to leave an oil stain on the page or on your apron, consider it a badge of honor.

Here's a great site for you: Cookpad.com

One of the largest recipe communities in the world, where users can share and discover new cooking ideas. The platform is available in many languages and offers recipes from every corner of the planet.

From Vine to Glass: An Ethyl Tour

If you thought your retirement was going to be one long coffee break, you forgot about the other liquid that makes the world go round: wine. But mind you, I'm not talking about the kind of wine that makes you sing love songs under your neighbor's window. I'm talking about the nectar that makes you see life through rose-colored glasses-or ruby ones, depending on the bottle.

While the Ethyl Tour may seem like an expedition reserved for the adventurous young, I assure you that no one has ever said, *"You're too old to taste a good Chianti."* In fact, with age, the palate becomes more refined, just like the intellect. And when your intellect tells you to avoid the stairs, listen to your palate when it whispers that you should try a Pinot Noir.

Let's start with the Old World, Europe, where the vine has flourished for millennia. If you choose Italy, I suggest you don't just stop at pizza and ice cream, Italian wine is appreciated all over the world! The wine regions of Tuscany, Piemonte and Veneto are home to such gems as Brunello di Montalcino, Barolo, and Prosecco. Not only will you taste excellent wines, but you will also find yourself walking among verdant hills and medieval castles, and maybe, just maybe, talking with your hands a little more than usual.

If your love of wine takes you over the Alps, France will welcome you with open arms, as long as you don't dare call every bubbly you encounter "champagne." The Loire Valley, Bordeaux, Burgundy -- names that make you dream. Here, every drop of wine tells a story, and if you stop and listen, you might even hear the vines whisper in the wind.

But the tour does not end here. Let's not forget Spain and its Tempranillo, or Portugal and its Port. And when you're ready to set foot in the New World, Argentina awaits with its Malbec, while California boasts its famous Cabernet Sauvignon and Zinfandel.

Now, I understand that this round-the-world wine trip may seem like a titanic mission. But who says you have to drink it all at once? The beauty of this ethyl tour is the journey itself, savoring each glass like a book, discovering the history, geography, and people behind each drop.

And if your journey doesn't take you beyond the couch, don't worry. There are plenty of wine shops and specialty stores that offer tastings and classes. Maybe you can organize a theme night with friends and family, where everyone brings a bottle from a different country. And in an instant, the world will come to you.

A wise old man (or maybe me on one of my ethyl nights) said, "*Life is too short to drink mediocre wines.*" So, raise your glass, my friend, and toast to retirement, to life, and to the journeys, real or imagined, that wine can offer you.

A well-done website is Vivino.com, where you can buy wines from all over the world and read customer reviews.

One last piece of advice: drink responsibly. You don't want to wake up in a vineyard trying to figure out how you got there - although, come to think of it, there are worse ways to start the day.

Themed Dinners: A World Tour in 80 Dishes

Ah, no, sorry - that's 7! Sure, Jules Verne took us around the world in 80 days. But going around the world in 80 dishes was too much, even for my memory. So, here's my suggestion: a world food tour, one dish for each continent. And when you start packing, please stop; all you need is an apron and good company.

1. Asia: Biryani
Biryani is not just spicy rice; it is a culinary work of art. Variations may vary from region to region, but every biryani has layers of fragrant basmati rice and marinated meat or vegetables, all slowly cooked to perfection. In some variations, you may even find prunes or hard-boiled eggs buried like treasures. And when you dig into its depths, every bite tells a story of centuries of refinement.

2. Africa: Moroccan Tagine
Tagine is not only a dish, but also the name of the traditional clay pot with a pointed lid. But inside? Oh, gentlemen. Tender lamb, sweet prunes, toasted almonds, and spices like saffron and turmeric. It's like biting into a cloud at sunset in the Sahara.

3. North America: Hamburger
A real hamburger is not just shredded meat between two slices of bread. It has nuance! The ideal is ground beef, cooked to perfection, topped with crisp lettuce, fresh tomato and, for the daring, a hint of onion. Oh, and let's not forget the secret sauce, which, like all secrets, makes life a little more mysterious.

4. South America: Peruvian Ceviche

Ceviche is not just raw fish. It is a dance of flavors: very fresh fish "cooked" in lemon juice, garnished with thinly sliced red onion, chopped cilantro, and a hint of chili pepper for heat. Some variations include crispy corn or sweet potatoes. It's like a crisp, fresh ocean on your plate!

5. Antarctica: Lemon Sorbet

Well, technically Antarctica does not have a traditional cuisine, but lemon sorbet was my idea! It is like a cool breeze on a hot summer day. It caresses the tongue with its sweet acidity and conjures up visions of vast frozen landscapes. Yes, I know I'm exaggerating, but let's continue.

6. Europe: Spanish Paella

Paella is a feast on a plate. Originating in Valencia, it combines rich yellow rice, succulent chunks of chicken or rabbit, a variety of seafood, and even green beans and red peppers. And that thin layer of crispy rice at the bottom of the pan? It's worth a trip just for that.

7. Oceania: Samoan Baked Chicken

Also known as "moamoa," this dish is full of tropical flavors. The chicken is marinated in a mixture of coconut milk, lime juice, soy sauce and local spices. When cooked, the chicken is tender and fragrant, evoking the essence of the Pacific Islands.

Each dish brings history, culture, and tradition. And while "Cookpad.com" will help you with the recipes, it is the adventure of tasting and sharing these dishes with friends that makes the culinary journey truly memorable.

6. Relationships: The True Elixir of Longevity

Relationships are those sweet human entanglements that make us less alone in this vast and sometimes bizarre theater of life. In the glorious chapter of retirement, when the days are finally ours and the ticking clock seems a little less hurried, we discover that the elixir of long life is not contained in some magic potion or hermetic vitamin jar. No, ladies and gentlemen, the real elixir is found in the warmth of friendly hands and shared smiles.

Oh, don't get me wrong, I'm not talking about comedy friendships where everyone is flawless, and the laughter is in the background. I'm talking about the real friendships, the ones with people who know your flaws and miraculously choose to hang out with you anyway! The friends who made fun of your disastrous cooking and laughed at your jokes when they were old-fashioned.

In post-work life, the art of socializing becomes an almost chivalrous endeavor. It involves discovering clubs where boredom is banished, telling jokes so old they are new, and cultivating new, old, and, why not, borrowed friendships!

And if you think retirement is a time to crawl into a corner, let me tell you, you are sorely mistaken! It's a time to lace up your dancing shoes, tune in to friendly frequencies, and discover that we're all a bit like good wine: we get better with age, and we're definitely better in good company!

Remember, life is a journey, and he who travels alone travels halfway. So, grab that glass of wine, join the chorus, tell a joke, and toast with whomever you like - that is the true elixir of long life!

Clubs: For Those Who Are Bored of Being Alone

Oh, my friend, you are looking at a world of social opportunities and adventure! There is a universe of clubs just waiting to be explored, a universe where the only limit is how much fun you are willing to have. Now get ready, because I'm about to reveal some of the best-kept secrets to never being alone again!

First, the magical world of Meetup: If you're wondering where to find your clan, let me introduce you to Meetup.com, an amazing site where souls come together in search of companionship and new experiences. It's like a friendship bazaar! Whether you are a painting enthusiast, a hiking lover, or an aspiring chef, Meetup is the key that unlocks all doors!

There are also specialized sites for each passion:
- **Chess.** If your ideal afternoons involve chess sets and pieces dancing in strategic battle, this site is your kingdom!
- **Lonely Planet.** For the intrepid traveler, Lonely Planet is the compass that guides you to unknown destinations and adventures in every corner of the globe.
- **Cookpad.** Browse recipes from around the world and share your culinary creations with other cooking enthusiasts!
- **Duolingo.** For the eternal language learner, a fun arena to hone your language skills with friends from around the world!

- **Behance.** A platform for creatives of all kinds, from designers to photographers, where you can share your portfolio and discover new talent.
- **Strava.** For those who love running, biking, and other outdoor sports, Strava is a place to track your performance and connect with other athletes.
- **Couchsurfing.** If you love to travel and meet locals, Couchsurfing connects you with people willing to share their home and culture.

But don't forget the local clubs. Okay, these virtual clubs are great! But don't underestimate the appeal of traditional clubs. The ones where the background noise is laughter, where hands shake and eyes sparkle with complicity. The ones where ideas cross paths and friendships are forged in the warm fire of sharing.

This is your town, your neighborhood, your community. Explore community centers, libraries, gyms. Discover walking groups, gardening circles, painting clubs. Be surprised by the diversity of people who, like you, are looking for companionship and new experiences.

Here are ten hidden gems:

- **The Sunset Painters' Academy.** A corner of the world where brush and paint bring masterpieces to life under fiery skies.
- **The Dawn Walkers.** For those who love to greet the sun and discover hidden paths while the world sleeps.
- **The Sudoku Warriors.** For those who find peace in the numerical battle of grids and squares.
- **The Brotherhood of Tales by the Fire.** A magical place where stories and legends come to life around a roaring fire.
- **The Eagles of Paragliding.** For those who seek the thrill and beauty of flying free in the sky.

- **The Pioneers of Homemade Bread**. A club for those who find joy and satisfaction in making their own bread with their own hands.
- **The Brotherhood of Wind Singing**. A group for those who love to sing and meet in open spaces to make their music resonate in nature.
- **The Legion of Bocce Players**. A meeting place for those who love this ancient game and are looking for opponents and friends to play with.
- **The Knights of the Poker Table**. A club for poker lovers, where strategy and luck meet.
- **The Convent of the Home Brewers**. A club for those who want to learn the art of home brewing and share their creations.

Each of us is a novel in the making, and each new encounter adds an unforgettable chapter to our story. Don't let fear stop you from discovering these clubs, making new friends, and writing amazing new episodes in your book of life!

I invite you to explore, to laugh, to learn, and most of all, to live! Retirement is not a sunset, but a bright dawn of opportunity and adventure. Who knows what wonderful treasures you will find and what friendships you will make along the way. Don't put off until tomorrow what you can do today!

Telling Jokes - And True Stories, Too

Telling jokes and stories is an art! Welcome to the stage of life where you can exaggerate the details, and no one will punish you. Now, my friend, I'm not talking about jokes you can read on a pack of tissues. I'm talking about stories that make you roll over with laughter and jokes that give you hiccups!

First secret: exaggerate! It's not about making things up; it's about making things more colorful. Was that fish you caught as big as your arm? Tell them it was as big as a whale, and they will see you as the fisherman of their dreams!

Every story has its moment. How about the one about meeting the bear? Perfect for an evening with friends, less so for a grandchild's christening. What about the jokes? The key is in the delivery. Pronounce them with the right tone, the right pause, and most importantly, that mischievous grin.

Where do you find this treasure trove of humor? Libraries, neighborhood bars, barbershops, storytelling clubs! Yes, there are clubs for those who, like you, love to tell stories. And don't forget the digital world! Sites like "Reddit" are gold mines for stories and jokes.

Storytelling is not just a way to pass the time. It is a way to connect, to share life, laughter, and sometimes tears. It is a way to pass on wisdom and keep traditions alive. You have many stories to tell, believe me!

So don't wait. Get out there, find your stories, perfect your jokes, and become the storyteller you've always wanted to be! And remember, a good story is worth a thousand words, but a good joke -- that one is priceless!

In this chapter of life, grab your storytelling stick and get ready to make the world laugh with your stories and jokes! Every laugh, every applause is a sign that you are living your best adventure, that of being a storyteller in the golden age of retirement!

New, Old, Borrowed Friends...

My friend, welcome to the chapter of life where you can collect friends like stamps! And if, like me, you always thought stamps were a bit boring, well, I assure you, friends are much more fun!

Let's start with old friends, the ones who know all your stories (and maybe even some of the most embarrassing ones). Cherish them like gold, because they know how to make you laugh by reminding you of the time... well, you know what I'm talking about!

But let's not stop there! Retirement is the perfect time to make new friends. And I'm not talking about those awkward encounters you had when you were young and had to invent an interesting hobby. No, now you can be yourself! Like collecting coasters? There's a club for that! Like walking in the park and talking to squirrels? You're not the only one! Making new friends may seem like a daunting task, but man, are you in a golden age of opportunity! Have you tried sites like Meetup.com? I've recommended it before - it's like a supermarket of friends where you can shop based on your interests. Whether you're a chess enthusiast, an accomplished cook, or a travel fanatic, you can find it all!

And then there are the borrowed friends. Yes, you read that right! These are your friends' friends, the ones you meet at parties and who make you think, "*Why haven't we met before?*" They're kind of like those books you borrow and don't want to return. But remember, sharing is love, don't keep them all to yourself!

Now, with all these new friends, you may ask, how do I keep track of them all? Well, my dear friend, this is where technology comes in. Fear not! Apps like "WhatsApp" and "Facebook" are

your allies. They help you stay in touch, share jokes and cat pictures, and plan your next adventure!
But a word of caution: don't let technology replace the real joy of companionship. Nothing beats a shared laugh, a warm hug, or that look of understanding that says, *"Oh yeah, I did that stupid thing too!"*

In the world of retirement, every day is an opportunity, and whether you're looking to rekindle old friendships, make new ones, or borrow a few friends here and there, remember the adage: *"He who finds a friend finds a treasure."*

7. Money With a Dash of Cunning

Ah, the bright and shiny topic everyone has been waiting for: money! But don't let appearances fool you, because my friend, let's talk about money, yes, but with a dash of cunning and cleverness!

Remember when you were young and thought money grew on trees? Well, if you had planted some money in the garden then, who knows, you might have a nice orchard now! But don't worry, it's never too late to make your money grow, and I'm not talking about planting it in the garden!

You've learned in life that all that glitters isn't gold, but who's to say you can't turn your silverware into a whole bunch of gold coins? And no, I'm not suggesting that you melt down your silverware! I'm talking about little tricks and gimmicks that can make your wallet a little plumper!

You'll see, with a few tricks on how to invest like a smart grandfather, how to use your passions for extra income, and how to balance your budget (see what I did there?), you'll find yourself laughing under your breath every time you open your wallet!

But don't get ahead of yourself! Before we dive into that golden sea, let's take a deep breath and prepare ourselves to navigate the waves of capital wisely.

After all, money doesn't make you happy, but a dash of cunning and a smile on your face can make the journey much more enjoyable!

The secret is not to have a full wallet, but a light heart and a head full of dreams.

Make Your Wallet Smile

My friend, when it comes to money, we all love a little magic. After all, who wouldn't want to find a $50 bill in a forgotten pocket? But if magic is not your thing, fear not! Here are some less magical (but just as effective) ways to put a smile on your overly serious wallet.

1. Get rid of unnecessary expenses. Take a look at those subscriptions you have: magazines, exotic food boxes, TV channels you never watch.... Do you really need all those magazines about growing cacti?
Analyze your bills: Call companies and ask for discounts, deals, or cheaper plans. People often forget that negotiating is not just for oriental bazaars.

2. Used stuff is the new "new". Markets, booths, and online sites like eBay: Buying used items not only saves money but is also environmentally friendly.
Trade or barter! Maybe your neighbor wants that old tennis racket and has a book you're interested in.

3. Save on food and drink. Avoid packaged foods and cook from scratch. Yes, I know it sounds like a celebrity chef trick, but I assure you, homemade risotto tastes better (and cheaper) than anything frozen.
Use apps like "Too Good To Go" to buy food at discounted prices as it nears its expiration date. Kill two birds with one stone: save money and reduce waste!

4. Become a discount code king or queen. There are websites that offer a myriad of coupons and discounts. It can feel like a treasure hunt, but in the end, the prize is real.
Sign up for newsletters from your favorite stores. Sure, they might fill up your inbox, but every once in a while, you might get that golden discount code!

5. Plan ahead. Holidays, parties, birthdays... The more you plan ahead, the more you save. Remember the adage "*You snooze, you lose?*" Well, it applies to saving too!
Consider buying tickets or gifts while they are on sale.

6. The power of self-education. Learn to do it yourself. Whether it's small household chores, sewing on a button, or baking bread, there are hundreds of online tutorials that can help. And if you end up with a boomerang loaf, at least you'll have a good story to tell!

7. Look to the future. Consider investing in more energy-efficient appliances or insulation for your home. It may seem expensive now but think of the savings in the long run!

8. Last but not least. Remember to budget. Yes, it may sound like something only accountants love, but keeping track of your expenses will help you understand where that "ghost" money is going.

Oh, and a little side note: The temptation to hide money under your mattress may be strong, but trust me, your wallet (and your back) will thank you for resisting that temptation.
These tips will make your grandfather proud, and your retirement... well, it will go a lot further than you thought. And now, happy saving, my friend! May the power of the Smiling Wallet be with you!

Invest Like a Smart Grandfather

Retiree, my friend, you've earned every penny of your pension, but who says we can't make it grow? Here are some tips on how to invest those savings with the wisdom of a wise grandfather and the enthusiasm of a kid in a candy store.

1. The value of gold
- Grandpa used to say, "*Gold is a man's best friend!*" Not literally, it can't give you advice or play cards, but it does hold its value over time.
- Buy gold coins, bars or invest in gold-related mutual funds.
- Crisis situations? Gold shines even brighter! It is a form of "safe haven" investment when others seem uncertain.

2. The art of investing in art
- Have you ever noticed that painting in the attic that Grandma thought was priceless? It might actually be!
- Frequent visits to auctions, art galleries and sites like Artmajeur can bring you closer to valuable pieces.
- Keep in mind that art is subjective, but a good Picasso has never let anyone down!

3. Real estate investments
- Buy, rent, sell. The game of Monopoly can become a reality!
- Consider buying property in developing or tourist areas.
- Remax is a great site to start your search, although the good old neighborhood tour never goes out of style.

4. Small businesses and start-ups
- Support young entrepreneurs! They are energetic, have innovative ideas, and you could get a piece of the action.

- A platform like "Kickstarter" allows you to discover innovative new projects.
- But be careful! It's risky, don't put all your eggs in one basket.

5. The stock market is not just a movie starring Leonardo DiCaprio
- Buying stocks can seem complicated, but with a little research and patience, you might just find your golden nugget.
- Use apps and websites like "Investing" to track stocks and stay on top of the market.
- Diversify! A little here, a little there, like an appetizer binge, you never know what you'll like best!

6. Green I want you to be green
- Invest in renewable energy and green companies. It's good for the planet and good for your wallet!
- Look for up-and-coming renewable energy and green technology companies.
- Bonus: Feeling good about doing something positive is a guaranteed extra return!

7. Become an urban farmer
- Invest in urban gardens or local agriculture projects. Not only will you contribute to the community, but you might even get some fresh produce in return!
- Research projects in your area that need funding or volunteers.
- Ah, the smell of the earth and the taste of vegetables grown with love! Priceless!

8. The importance of education.
- We never stop learning. Invest in courses and training to gain new skills.

- The Udemy platform offers courses on a variety of topics.
- Who knows, you might discover a hidden passion or, why not, start a second career!

9. Save for your grandchildren.
- Consider starting a savings fund or investment plan for your grandchildren.
- Not only will you help them in the future, but you will also make Mom and Dad happy!

10. Retirement and Security.
- Even if you are already retired, it may be helpful to have a supplemental retirement plan or life insurance.
- Research the options and choose the one that best meets your and your family's needs.

Remember, all investments involve risk. Grandpa used to say, *"Don't run faster than your legs!"* Do your research, seek advice, be patient, and most importantly, enjoy the process. After all, investing is a bit like fishing: you never know what you're going to catch, but every once in a while, you might catch a big one! Good luck, my friend, and may the wise grandfather in your guide your financial decisions!

When Passion Turns to Profit

There is an inner fire that makes us jump out of bed in the morning; it is passions. Well, my friend, today we are going to explore how to turn your hobbies into thriving businesses, because as Grandpa used to say, *"There is no sweeter work than work you love!"*

1. **Art and Creativity**.
    - Are you a hidden artist? Now is the time to sell your creations on platforms like "Etsy" where crafts and art meet buyers from all over the world!
    - Tip: Always sign your work! You never know when you might become famous!

2. **Cooking and Gastronomy**.
    - Are your cookies driving the neighborhood crazy? Try selling them at the local market or create a cookbook.
    - Next Step: Online cooking lessons! Share your secret recipes - for a small fee, of course!

3. **Write and blog**.
    - Even if your biography didn't sell millions of copies, you can still be successful with a blog! You can create one on the popular "WordPress" platform.
    - Write about what you love, whether it's fishing, sewing, or stamp collecting. There is an audience for everything!
    - Also check out Facebook and Twitter.

4. **Antiques and collectibles**.
    - If your attic looks like a museum and you know the difference between "old junk" and "vintage treasures," you may have a gold mine in your home! Sites like eBay or Catawiki are perfect for selling these items.
    - Offer your expertise as an appraiser or consultant. Many people are looking for experts who can tell a fake from the real thing.

5. **Photography and video**.
    - If your camera is your best friend, sell your photos on sites like Shutterstock or Depositphotos.
    - Create a YouTube channel and share your photography adventures.

6. **Teaching and tutoring**.
    - Have a deep knowledge of a subject? Teach on platforms like Udemy or Preply.
    - Give private lessons in your community. Not only will you make some money, but you'll be making a difference in someone's life!

7. **Music and entertainment**.
    - If you play an instrument, why not teach it? Or create your own music and sell it on Discogs.
    - Organize music events in your community. A karaoke night or a backyard concert can be a source of income!

8. **Sports and Fitness**.
    - If you are fit and love sports, why not start a fitness blog or vlog? Platforms like "WordPress" for blogs and "YouTube" for vlogs are multilingual and reach a global audience!

My friend, the secret is to do what you love and share it with others. It's not just about making a few bucks; it's about sharing your passion and inspiring others. Go for it if you want to turn your passion into profit!

Budgets Without Scales

There was once a retiree who said, "*My budget is like a broken scale, it always wobbles!*" But don't despair, my friend! Even if it seems like your money has grown wings and is trying to escape from your wallet, I am here to tell you that there are ways to make sure your budget does not wobble like a broken scale.

1. **The art of budgeting in a nutshell**
   - Make a list of your income: You have multiple sources of income. From pensions to odd jobs, write it all down. Don't forget the neighbor who pays you in apple pies for mowing the lawn!
   - Track your expenses: Okay, I know it sounds boring, but tracking your expenses doesn't mean you have to become an accountant. All you need is a small planner or maybe an app on your smartphone to keep track of everything.
   - Cut out the unnecessary: There are expenses that seem unavoidable, like that gardening magazine you never read. Or the gym you only go to for the free coffee. Cut these unnecessary expenses and see how much you save!

2. **Little tricks that make a big difference**
   - Schedule your savings: Set up an automatic transfer from your checking account to your savings account each month. Even $10 a month adds up to $120 a year! Not bad for dinner out.
   - Reduce your energy use: I'm not suggesting you live in the dark, but turning off the lights when you leave a room or turning down the heat a degree can make a difference in your utility bills. As a bonus, you are helping the environment!

3. **Turn spending into revenue**
   - Loyalty programs: There are many loyalty cards that offer discounts or points for every purchase. And yes, I know what you're thinking, *"But I already have a wallet full of cards!"* But some are really worth it. American Express, for example, is a card with a great loyalty program.

- Sell what you don't use: Those old vinyls you have in your attic could be worth a fortune! Or maybe that bicycle you no longer use. Sites like "eBay" can help you sell things you no longer use.

4. Financial counseling
- If all else fails, consider consulting a financial advisor. Many offers free initial consultations.

Retirement does not mean you have to watch every penny. But with a little planning and a few smart tricks, you can make your money work for you. If you can't fix a broken budget, you can certainly make sure your budget stays balanced!

8. Fit, Although Round Is a Fit

My friend, I've always told myself that when nature decided to shape the human form, it did so with a sense of humor. And if you look in the mirror and see that your shape is more like a ball than an arrow, don't worry! Remember that the earth, with all its charms and wonders, is round, and no one seems to complain about that.

But when you look at your round, shiny shadow, you may wonder how you can keep this magnificent body moving, especially now that you have all the time in the world to take care of yourself. Well, fear not, because we have a few tips for you! After all, it's not just about how you feel, it's also about how you move. And if nothing else, we will move through these pages together, laughing at our curves and contortions as we try to stay in shape.

Before we dive into the meanderings of cerebral crosswords and yoga-logic contortions, remember one thing: every little movement counts. If you decided to get off the couch just to grab another cookie, congratulations, you just got a mini workout! And while you're enjoying that cookie, think about all the physical and mental adventures we're going to explore together.

Get ready to discover that "being fit" is not just for the young and buff, but also for the wise and chubby like us!
Now, take a deep breath (not too deep, we don't want you to get tired right away) and get ready to dive into the art of staying fit, no matter how fit you are!

Puzzles and Crosswords: The Gym of the Mind

When I was younger, I imagined that the "gym of the mind" was a place where people lined up to lift weights with large volumes of encyclopedias. Ah, such laughter! But as you well know, my friend, mind training does not require gym clothes or sweat. Most importantly, it does not involve record-breaking lifts with heavy tomes. The brain, like any other muscle, needs regular exercise. And don't worry, I'm not suggesting that you do advanced math (unless you want to!).

Have you ever wondered why puzzles and crosswords are so popular with smart people like us? It's not just because they're fun, or because they're the ideal option when television decides to betray us with its usual soap operas. It's because they're a gym for the mind, a way to keep it active and agile.

Why do puzzles and crosswords?
- For fun: The laughter you feel when you finally find that word you've been missing is priceless.
- Mental agility: You exercise your problem-solving skills and improve your memory.
- Learning: Hey, how many new terms or trivia have you learned as a result?

Let's start with the right approach:
1. Choose the right difficulty level: If you are a beginner, start with easier puzzles. As you get better, you can increase the difficulty.
2. Find the right place: Good lighting and a comfortable chair can make all the difference.

3. **Establish a routine:** Set aside some time each day to do your puzzle or crossword. It can be a great afternoon break or a relaxing activity before bed.

Where to find puzzles and crosswords?
- Magazines and newspapers: Many have special sections, some with varying levels of difficulty.
- Specialized books: There are entire publications devoted to puzzles and crosswords. You can find them in any physical or digital bookstore.
- Websites: Websites such as "Jigsaw Planet" or "Devarai" offer a wide range of puzzles and crosswords.

Practical tips for doing crosswords and puzzles:
- Don't rush: Remember that this is a mental exercise, not a race.
- Use a pen with erasable ink: Ah, the satisfaction of erasing and correcting a mistake!
- Ask for help: If you get stuck, ask for help. Maybe from your neighbor or that nephew who knows everything.
- Don't beat yourself up: If you can't complete a puzzle, move on to the next one. The important thing is to have fun!

One last tip to remember: As with any workout, consistency is key. There is no need to overdo it one day and then forget about it for a week. Less is more!

"The mind may grow old, but it must never grow rusty." And with these puzzles and crosswords, I guarantee it will be as shiny as a new silver coin!

Dance and Yoga: Bending Without Breaking

Oh, my friend, have you reached the age where you feel like your bones are playing hide-and-seek every time you try to move? Well, let me tell you a secret: even in your 20s, you have those days. But let's move on. Before you indulge in the sedentary chair routine, try bending your body, not your will!

1. The art of dancing without looking like a crazy puppet
- Pick a dance: Choose slow, rhythmic dances like the waltz or tango. You can try break dancing but ask yourself if you really want to be famous in the hospital.
- Learn the basic steps: First, learn the music. Count the beats and move in time. Two left, two right. Nothing too complicated.
- Online lessons: I recommend YouTube, where you can find video tutorials and explanations for all levels.
- The right shoes: A good pair of dance shoes can mean the difference between "I danced all night" and "I need a chiropractor."

2. Yoga: Lean forward without looking back
The myth is that age and flexibility are mortal enemies, but don't let that fool you. Who says a retiree can't touch her toes without passing out?
- Start with the basics: Don't go straight for the lotus position if your best effort so far has been avoiding stains on the couch. Poses like "The Cat," "The Dog," and "The Tree" are a good place to start.
- Special mat: Use a non-slip mat, but if you want to be daring, do yoga on the carpet. Just remember to put it in the washing machine afterwards!

- Watch the class: Again, start with YouTube, you will find many tutorials for all levels, from beginner to advanced.
- Listen to your body: If your body is telling you, "*Hey, this bend is not for me,*" listen to it. You don't want to end up Googling "yoga emergency doctors."

So, what have we learned today?
1. Whether you can dance or bend like a contortionist, the important thing is to have fun and not try to impress your neighbor (unless you're trying to win her over!).
2. Age is just a number. Willpower is something you cultivate.
3. Whatever you choose, dance or yoga, remember that movement is life. And if you don't believe me, try sitting still for five minutes without thinking about cake or cookies!

Finally, my friend, I suggest you enjoy every movement and remember that with your wisdom and years of experience, you can certainly do better than a clumsy beginner. Have fun and don't forget to bend over (without collapsing, mind you)!

Healthy Eating: More Enjoyment, Less Dieting

When I was a young scion, I thought "healthy eating" was a euphemism for "tasteless eating." Oh, how wrong I was! Now that you've lived long enough to know that fish is better than fast food, and that a salad is not just for rabbits, read on to find out how to really enjoy eating well!

1. The legend of "ancient food"
Once upon a time, in a time long ago, bananas were straight and carrots were not orange, foods that are now considered "superfoods". Yes, exactly!
- **Quinoa**. This little grain is so high in protein; it will make you forget you need meat!
- **Kale**. Also known as collard greens. Rich in vitamins and minerals, it's perfect for salads and smoothies. And please, try it before you say you don't like it.

2. False friends of your belly
All that glitters is not gold, and my friend, that includes food.
- **Refined Sugar**. It has more disguises than a jewel thief. It hides in soft drinks, desserts, and sauces. A golden rule? If it sounds like chemistry, it probably is. Read the labels!
- **Fried foods.** Mmm, the French fries! How we love them. But what about your heart? Not really. Opt for baked or grilled versions.

3. The wonders of water-and no, I'm not talking about swimming
Drinking water may seem obvious, but I'm not talking about drinking two glasses and then replacing the rest with coffee and wine.
- **Flavored water**. Add cucumber slices, mint, or berries for a touch of flavor. You might be surprised at how much water you drink in a day.
- **Green tea**. Rich in antioxidants, it helps burn fat. But beware, it also contains some caffeine. Don't drink it before bedtime unless you want to count sheep until dawn.

4. The sweet sin you can't resist
Sweets are a part of life, but who says milk chocolate is the only way to get your dose of happiness?

- **Dark chocolate**. Rich in antioxidants and much lower in sugar. You can even pretend to be a gourmet by talking about the cacao content.
- **Dried fruit**. Plums, apricots, dates-the sweetness of nature!

And now some golden tips (and I'm not talking about carrots):
1. **Variety.** Eat the rainbow! I'm not talking about sweets; I'm talking about fruits and vegetables. The more colors you have on your plate, the better.
2. **Portions.** You don't need to be a mathematician but know that your eye is bigger than your stomach. Eat slowly and listen to your body.
3. **Avoid pre-cooked foods**. Especially those foods that look like they came out of a science experiment.

My friend, remember that healthy eating does not mean sacrificing taste or pleasure. It just means making better choices, sipping that bottle of water with a hint of pride, and smiling knowing you cheated the system by eating well and enjoying every bite. *"Life is too short to eat boring food!"*

Meditation: Silence - Time to Clear Your Mind!

Welcome to what may seem like a wonderland for your mind, but without the mad hatter. Although, come to think of it, with all the thoughts you've accumulated over the years, maybe there's already a mad hatter living in there!

Meditation: A Brief Overview

Have you ever noticed how children can stare at an ant for hours, completely absorbed? Meditation is more or less like that, except without the ant. But if the ant helps you, why not use it?

Start with the breath (or what's left of it):
1. **Find a quiet place.** I'm not talking about the secret room where you hide the cookies, but a place without distractions.
2. **Sit comfortably.** On the floor, on the chair, on the couch, on the cloud.... OK, maybe not the cloud.
3. **Close your eyes and begin to focus on your breath.** Imagine each inhalation as a new experience and each exhalation as a forgotten old joke.

Tools to help you:
- **Meditation app**: The Serenity app can help; it provides step-by-step instructions. And no, it won't ask you to say "Ommm" unless you want to!
- **Soothing music**: Although, let's face it, that old Frank Sinatra tape might work just as well.

Small steps to great silence:
1. Start with 5 minutes a day: You don't become a monk in a day. Unless you accidentally enter a monastery.
2. Pick a time: Preferably not when your favorite TV show is about to start.
3. Be patient: If your mind wanders, let it. Maybe it's just a craving for ice cream.

But what to eat? Does meditation have a menu?
Ah! A wise question. Although meditation does not have a set menu, there are some foods that can help put your mind in a Zen state:
- Chamomile tea: Calms and relaxes. Just make sure you don't fall asleep before you start meditating.
- Nuts and seeds: Rich in omega-3s, they help keep your brain sharp. And, no, it won't turn into a rubber band.
- Red fruits: Rich in antioxidants, they help keep your mind fresh and clear. But skip the ice cream.
- Avoid coffee and sugar before meditation: Unless you want to meditate on a sugar high.

Also, drinking plenty of water and eating light can help you maintain a sense of lightness as you wind through the meanders of your mind.

Meditation is not a race. There are no prizes for those who finish first, only the gift of inner peace. And unless you want to trade that peace for a good old-fashioned chocolate cake (I don't blame you!), I suggest you hold on to it.

My friend, in the silence of the mind you can find answers to questions you didn't even know you had. And if it all sounds like a lot of hogwash, well, at least you've spent a few minutes in silence. And in these times, that is a great accomplishment!

9. The Digital: A Domesticated World

There it is the digital world! Once a wilderness populated by basement nerds with glasses as thick as bottle bottoms, it has surprisingly become the good new living room of retirees. I know you kind of miss the thunder of the old typewriter keys, but now you can write me an entire letter - without even touching a piece of paper. That's the magic of technology!

Remember the days when you had to wait a week for a letter to get to know a person? Now, with one click, you can find out everything about your aunt's life, from the color of her new cat to her last trip to Patagonia. All while you're sitting on your couch in your pajamas.

But don't worry! I don't want to turn you into one of those young people glued to their phones. Instead, I want to guide you through the wonders of the digital world without making you feel like a fish out of water. And in between clicks, you might even learn how to post that picture of your lunch that everyone's dying to see.

In short, my friend, I will help you tame this new "animal" called digital. That way, the next time your grandson tells you to "scroll up" or "double click," you can proudly reply, "*I already know that!*" and maybe even show him a trick or two.

Get ready to take a (not too big) leap into the future! Here's your guide to taming the digital beast and having it sit politely next to you while you sip your afternoon tea.

Navigating the Web Without Getting Shipwrecked

Surfing the Web is a bit like setting sail in the middle of the open sea in a boat you have never steered before. You may even find yourself battling a mermaid in the form of misleading advertisements inviting you to click on them. But fear not! With the right compass and a map in my hand (or rather, on my keyboard), I will guide you on this voyage overseas without soaking your socks.

Browser boat: First, you need to choose your boat, or in this case, your "browser." Chrome, Firefox, Edge--these are just a few of the names you may have heard your grandson grumble about. Each has its own quirks. Try them all and choose the one you feel most comfortable with. It's like choosing a chair: if you fall asleep in it within five minutes, it's the one!

Knots and anchors favorites: Now that you've got your browser up and running, it's time to learn how to tie a nautical knot: save your favorite sites. That way, when you want to go back and read the latest gossip about that famous actor of your day, or maybe just check the weather, you can do it with one click. No, we're not talking about magic, just a feature called "favorites" or "bookmarks."

Beware the rocks - online scams: Just like the open sea, there are hidden dangers. Not all sites are friendly. But here's a good rule of thumb: If a site promises you money in exchange for your email or phone number... well, my friend, chances are there's a catfish on the hook. And I'm not talking about the kind you can fry.

Fishing for information - Google and search engines: Think of Google as your fishing buddy. Type what you are looking for into the search bar, et voila! Google will pull up a net full of information. But be careful: as with fish, fresh information is best. Avoid clicking on old links or sites with strange names. What if a site asks you to download something? Well, if you don't know what you're doing, it's best to send the fish back to the sea.

Treasure maps – cookies: Have you ever heard of "cookies" without referring to those delicious sweets? In the world of the Web, cookies are little bits of data that Web sites use to remember your preferences. They are like treasure maps that help you find your way back. But some maps can lead you into a trap. So, it is always a good idea to clean up your cookies from time to time. How do I do that? No, you don't need a vacuum cleaner, there is an option in your browser settings, just find it.

Bottled messages – email: Email is like sending messages in bottles, but much, much faster. But be careful not to open every bottle that arrives! Some may contain letters from hackers. If you receive a suspicious email or one that asks for personal information, throw it away. It's not worth the risk of shipwreck.

Surfing the Web may seem like a titanic task, but with a little caution and a few tips, you'll soon be the captain of your own ship. There is no need to sail alone, ask for help when you need it, and you will soon find that the digital sea holds no secrets for you!

Social Networks: Jokes and Pictures of Cats

There are digital places where everyone has an opinion, and most of them are convinced that the world can't help but hear it-that's social networking. But if you are like me, you prefer to use these strange collections of pixels to share a good laugh or admire the latest acrobatic feat of the neighbor's cat.

Remember when jokes were told at the local bar or country club? Well, now they're all over Facebook, Instagram, and everywhere else. And if you're wondering if you should share that picture of your cat doing a handstand on the edge of the bathtub, the answer is yes. Absolutely yes.

How to choose your digital town square: There are a lot of social networks out there, but not all of them are created equal. Facebook is like the town square, where you can find everything from serious news to silly jokes. Instagram, on the other hand, is like an art gallery for photos. What about Twitter? Well, think of it as a big marketplace where everyone is shouting at the same time. Choose your spot based on what you like to do: laugh, watch, listen.

From spectator to actor: Once you've chosen your digital stage, it's time to take the stage. Want to tell a joke? Go for it! But remember, humor may change, but good taste does not. Avoid topics that are too controversial. Otherwise, be prepared to receive comments from people who have nothing better to do than argue online. And, my friend, it's not worth it.

Cats, dogs, and parrots: I don't know why, but the Internet is crazy about animals. And if you have a pet, you're already halfway to becoming a social celebrity. But a word of advice: make sure your furry (or feathered) friend is cool with it before you post.

Netiquette, or the art of online civility: As in real life, there are unwritten rules online. Don't shout (i.e., don't write everything in ALL CAPS). Don't interrupt conversations. And above all, if you don't have anything good to say, don't say anything at all.

Oh, and if someone bothers you, there is always the magic "block" or "report" button. Use it wisely.

Connect and reconnect: One of the great things about social networking is that you can reconnect with old friends. That old flame from middle school? She's probably posting pictures of her grandkids. Your old coworker? He's probably sharing jokes just like you. Reconnecting can be fun but remember: the past is the past for a reason.

Protect your privacy: Despite the laughs and cat pictures, social networks are public places. Don't share information that's too personal and check your privacy settings. You wouldn't want your phone number in the hands of a vacuum cleaner salesman, would you?

Social networks can be a great place for fun and connection. But as with any adventure, it's best to be prepared. And as always, when in doubt, ask a grandchild. They like to feel useful every now and then.

Apps: Little Helpers Hidden in Your Phone

When I was young, the words "Apple" and "Android" conjured up images of fresh fruit and movie robots. Now they are synonymous with smartphone operating systems. And if you're thinking, *"What does an apple have to do with a phone?"* well, I get it. The modern world has its own unique way of confusing us.

You see, today's phones are like Swiss army knives: multifunctional. But unlike a pocketknife, there's no risk of cutting yourself. These technological marvels can do almost anything, thanks to little programs called "apps." Here's a guide to understanding these digital creatures and how they can make your life easier.

Apps for everyday life:
- **Evernote**. For keeping track of everything. From grocery lists to dentist appointment reminders to joke ideas for the next social gathering.
- **Shazam.** How many times have you heard a song on the radio and wondered what it's called? Well, Shazam "listens" to the song and tells you. It's like having a music expert in your pocket.
- **Trello.** A kind of virtual bulletin board where you can pin things to do, ideas, projects. And as a bonus, no risk of getting stuck with thumbtacks.

An app for having fun (and being a little vague):
- **Audible**. Listen to audiobooks. If reading tires your eyes or hands, let someone else do it for you!
- **Spotify**. A digital jukebox. Although you might miss the sound of coins .... special, you know?
- **Sketchbook.** Draw, color, and express your creativity.
- **TuneIn Radio**. Radio stations from around the world and podcasts on every topic you can imagine. Even ones you might not have thought of.

Apps for getting fit (or trying to):
- **MyFitnessPal**. Helps you track what you eat. Perfect for those who love pizza but don't want to feel guilty.
- **Calm**. Guided meditation. For when the world gets a little too loud. Shape. Just seven minutes, so no excuses!
- **Meditopia**. Guided meditation for mind and soul. Imagine you are on a beach, the waves are lapping...

App for traveling (without getting lost):
- **Google Maps**. Show you the way. And if you get lost, it will find you. But there is no guarantee that it will always take you to the right place. Let's face it, who among us hasn't followed a GPS down a mysterious little street?
- **TripAdvisor**. Advice on where to eat, where to sleep, and what to do. But take it with a grain of salt. Remember, one person might hate what another loves.
- **XE Currency**. Find out how much your money is worth in another country. And find out that, yes, that ceramic cat figurine was really overpriced.
- **AccuWeather**. Detailed weather forecasts. Although the rain will still catch you when you least expect it.

Security app (because a little paranoia never hurts):
- **LastPass**. Remembers your passwords for you. And trust me, it's a lot more reliable than the list hidden under your keyboard.
- **bSafe**. Sends an emergency message with your location to people you trust if you feel you are in danger.
- **Norton Mobile Security**. Keeps your device safe from viruses and other threats. Because attackers don't just look in your drawers, they sometimes sneak into your phone.

App for the curious and learning enthusiast:
- **Wikipedia**. The encyclopedia of the modern world. Although taking everything you read as gospel may not be the idea of the century.
- **Google Lens**. Point it at something you don't recognize, and it tells you what it is. Kind of like having a know-it-all nephew around all the time, but without the sarcastic comments.

- **TED**. Short talks on fascinating topics. For when you feel intellectual but don't want to read a whole book.

And now, the app superstars you can't miss:
- **WhatsApp**. For texting, calling, and sending photos. And for those cute cat videos your sister sends you.
- **Facebook**. Where everyone shares photos, stories, and recipes. And the occasional political discussion. Every now and then.
- **Instagram**. For those who love photos. And for those who like to apply filters to photos to make them look like they were taken in another decade.
- **Google Drive**. Store your documents, photos, and more. It's like having a locker in your phone.
- **YouTube**. Videos of all kinds. From recipes to tutorials to kittens. Especially kittens.
- **Amazon**. For those days when you want to shop without leaving the house. And yes, you probably need that cat pillow set.

And there are many, many more... Apps can be great tools if you use them wisely. They are like potatoes: they may seem weird and wrinkly at first, but once you get to know them, they become an integral part of your tech diet. And if you ever run into trouble, well, there's always an app for that! And if there isn't, ask a grandchild. They are like little living encyclopedias of these things.

10. Leave a Footprint (Without Making a Mess)

If we could see the world from a cloud (perhaps with the help of a few glasses of wine, we can), we would notice the incessant flow of life. People running here and there, engaged in a thousand affairs, from the seemingly mundane to the profoundly philosophical. And in the midst of all these frenetic beings, there we are, the glorious retirees, looking at the world with wise eyes and a touch of mischief.

Now, the world would have us believe that once we reach retirement, our imprint on the world becomes less profound, almost like a gentle breeze brushing the leaves. But, my friend, this could not be further from the truth! In fact, retirement is our great moment. It is the moment when we can finally make a difference without the constraints of the clock whispering insistently in our ear. Without littering, of course. No one wants to be famous for spilling soup on grandma's new tablecloth.

To leave a footprint is to contribute, to create, to surprise, and in some way to be eternally present. Not in the ghostly sense, but in the sense of a legacy. And no, I'm not talking about leaving your mark on history like Napoleon or Cleopatra. Although, let's face it, it would be fun to see yourself on a coin or have a cocktail with your name on it.

The idea is much simpler and more human. It is about sharing what we know, helping others, creating something that lives beyond us. Maybe a recipe, maybe a story, maybe just a small gesture that makes the world a better place. Let's see how you can become a master of this noble art!

Writing Memories, Even Fictional Ones

Ah, memory! That faithful companion that has a habit of turning into a somewhat absent-minded lady as the years go by. One day you remember exactly how Grandma's cake tastes, and the next you wonder where you left your car keys. Or, in your case, where you parked the car. But I'm afraid that's another story.
I don't want to belittle your memory. After all, you have collected a treasure trove of anecdotes and adventures along your life's journey. And yes, maybe some details got lost along the way, but it is in those moments that your creativity can shine. Why not mix reality with fantasy and breathe new life into your memories?

Imagine you are writing your own journal. "Dear memory," you might begin, "*Do you remember the time I won a fencing tournament in France?*" You may never have held a sword, but who knows? And even if someone were to suspect, you would simply respond with a mysterious, "*Ah, those were wild times!*"

The truth is that memories are like wine: some get better with age, others ... well, they become something else entirely. And who is to say which version is better? Certainly not me, and neither can you. The important thing is that you enjoy yourself and bring a smile to the faces of those who read your adventures, real or imagined.

But you may ask, "*Why should I write my memories?*" Well, let me give you a few reasons. First, it is a way to get your mind in order. Sometimes putting your experiences on paper can help you see things from a different perspective, rediscover happy moments you had forgotten, or find a new perspective on less pleasant episodes.

Second, writing down your memories (and inventions) is a valuable gift to those around you. Your grandchildren, or your friends' grandchildren, may discover that Grandpa or Grandma were living legends, even if the most heroic episode of your day was actually the time you saved your sandwich from the clutches of a hungry pigeon.

Then there is the sheer joy of writing. Maybe you'll discover you have a hidden talent, or maybe you just enjoy playing with words. And don't worry if you don't think you're good enough: there are plenty of resources to help you, including books, writing classes, and, of course, your own insatiable imagination.

After all, writing down your memories, real or imagined, is a way to leave your mark on the world, a legacy of stories and adventures. And who knows, maybe someday, many years from now, someone will find your journal in an old attic and discover a world full of magic, adventure, and, yes, a few innocents little lies. But as I've always said, a little lie in the name of good storytelling never hurt anyone!

DIY: Everything Deserves a Second Life

Bricolage is an art! That delightful practice that transforms what seems destined for the dustbin into something extraordinarily unique. Those objects that, with a little love and care, can be reborn and blossom into a new adventure.

1. Why DIY?
First, let's take a step back and consider why DIY holds a place of honor in the hearts of so many.

- **Savings**. While not all of us were born with silver in our mouths, DIY allows us to create golden objects with what we have on hand.
- **Creativity**. Your mind is a well of ideas; it's time to mine it and make it shine!
- **Environment**. Bringing objects back to life not only makes you feel good, it's good for the planet. And remember, climate change is real, no matter what your old friend says.

2. What you need to get started:
- **Essential Tools**: A collection of basic tools like a hammer, screwdriver, pliers, and of course, duct tape (or as I call it, the Little Emergency Wizard).
- **Materials**: Anything you have around the house that you were going to throw away. Yes, even that old teapot with no lid.
- **Inspiration**: A platform like Pinterest can give you ideas for DIY projects you never imagined. But if you prefer something more traditional, find a local library or bookstore. Their DIY sections are full of hidden gems.

3. Easy ideas and projects to get you started:
Turn old T-shirts into reusable bags
1. Get an old T-shirt.
2. Cut off the sleeves and neck.
3. Sew or knot the bottom.
4. Et Voila! You have a new tote bag.

Make candleholders from old cups
1. Get an old mug.
2. Place a candle inside.
3. You can also decorate the mug with paint or ribbon.

4. When things get complicated:
Hey, no one said this was going to be easy! But as any good sailor knows, there is always a calm after the storm. Here are some tips for navigating the turbulent waters of DIY:
- **Be patient**: Not everything will work on the first try. But as my grandmother used to say, if it doesn't work, try again!
- **Ask for help**: Home improvement groups, Web sites, and even your neighbor who converted his garage into a workshop may have the advice you're looking for.
- **Remember why you're doing it**: Not just to save money or the environment, but for yourself. For the sheer joy of creating.

5. Advanced:
If you're feeling really adventurous and tired of beginner projects, why not try something more challenging? You could create recycled furniture, jewelry, or even artwork!

The DIY journey is like life itself. There will be ups and downs, moments of joy and frustration. But at the end of the day, you will have something beautiful and unique, just like you.

Making Plans, Even Without a Plan

Get comfortable, my friend. We are about to enter the maze of projects. Yes, you read that right: making projects without a real project in mind. Sound like a crazy idea? Well, remember when you were younger and wanted to be an astronaut, a flamenco dancer, or maybe the first knight of a modern round table? Here we go again, only this time with less hair and more experience!

1. The power of improvisation
Sometimes a well-defined plan can be the enemy of creativity. It's like trying to fit a camel into a matchbox. And by the way,

don't try that last trick; it never ends well for you, the camel, or the box.

- Sit in a comfortable place. It could be that old chair you spilled your coffee on last year.
- Get a piece of paper and a pen.
- Write down whatever is on your mind. Yes, anything. Even your favorite lasagna recipe.

Now look at that list. It probably looks like the delirium of a drunken parrot. But it is your delirium, and there is beauty in it.

2. Where do ideas come from?
From everything! From a conversation with the mailman, from a cloud that looks vaguely like Abraham Lincoln, or from the way your cat looks at you as if it were about to give you an important assignment.
Tip: Look at the world around you as if you were seeing it for the first time. Imagine that you are an explorer on a new planet. Earth, the planet of surprises!

3. Give us a direction (even if it is in a circle)
Now that you have a list (or collage) of ideas, choose something that stands out to you. It doesn't matter if it sounds ridiculous.

- Put yourself out there. Want to write a short story? Start with a sentence. Want to paint? Make a brush stroke. Be your own number one fan. Laugh at your own ideas but remember that every great work of art began as a seemingly crazy idea.
- Share it! Show it to your friends, family, or the bartender down the street. Their laughter or advice may give you a new perspective.

4. Don't get discouraged
If you hit a dead end, take a break. Sometimes the best ideas come when you least expect them, like during a long shower or when you're looking in vain for your house keys.

5. Celebrate small victories
Wrote a five-line poem about your favorite socks? Great. Draw a picture of your goldfish that looks more like a penguin? Even better! The important thing is that you created something.

Remember, life itself is one big project with no definite plan. And you have sailed through it like an experienced captain, facing storms and calm waters with equal passion. So why not do the same with your plans? In the end, you may find that the real project was the journey itself and the laughter you collected along the way.

Renaissance of the Retiree: From Sage to Guide

Who said the Renaissance ended in the 17th century? In fact, you, my friend, could be the beginning of a new Renaissance. And no, I'm not talking about wearing tights and a feathered hat, although? well, that would definitely be a sight to behold!

Acknowledge Your Wisdom. Years of experience cannot be packaged and shipped (and if you try, let me know how it goes). You have lived, laughed, cried, and most importantly, learned. So how does a retiree turn this wisdom into guidance? **Offer your life lessons**. Everyone makes mistakes. Yes, even you. The difference between you and a guy who slips on ice for the first time is that you have slipped hundreds of times. And you know how to avoid falling again. You give advice when asked. You might even start a little blog or, for the less digitally savvy, a monthly column at the condo meeting. But be careful: always give advice, not scold like candy on Halloween.

Become a mentor. Find a young protégé (or even two or three, if you're feeling energetic). I am not suggesting that you take on an apprentice like a fairy tale wizard, but that you help someone in their career or passion. This can be done either formally, by joining a mentoring program, or informally, by helping the kid next door who is struggling with his new hobby.

Share your story. Even if you have lived an ordinary life, there are bound to be episodes of hilarity, wisdom, and introspection. Share these stories. You can do this in a class, a seminar, or, why not, a storytelling night at your favorite club.

Join groups and organizations. You never know when you might be the only person who knows how to fix that antique cuckoo clock or solve that math puzzle. Your expertise could be invaluable to groups like the Lions Club, local library, or neighborhood association.

Never stop learning. To be a guide, you must also be a student. You may know all about 1960s cars, but why not learn something new like digital photography or painting? This will make you a master of the new as well as the old.

Wisdom is like wine: it improves with age. But unlike wine, it does not need to be locked away in a cellar. Be generous with your experience, share your knowledge, and you may find that this stage of your life is not twilight, but a new, radiant dawn. So, while the world celebrates artists like Leonardo da Vinci or Michelangelo, perhaps one day they will celebrate you. And who knows, in the future, history books may include your name among the great names of the Renaissance: "*The retiree who started the new Renaissance!*"

The End? Just a New Beginning!

My friend, if you have made it this far, it means that you have spent the last few hours (or days, depending on your reading speed) immersed in this guide. And now you may be asking yourself, "*So what? What happens next?*" Well, the answer is simple: whatever you want!

You are at the end of a book, but on the eve of an incredible adventure. This "retirement" we have been talking about is not an arrival station, but a launching pad. So tie your shoes (or put on those comfortable slippers, if you prefer) and get ready!

Life, Retirement and Looking Forward to the Next Adventures!

Life has never ceased to amaze you, has it? You've seen the birth of new technologies, the evolution of fashion (some of which, I bet, you hoped would never come back), and you've collected stories that could fill libraries. Retirement is not a pause to watch the world go by. It is an opportunity to open it up, jump out, and ask yourself, "*Where is the wind taking me today?*"

Retirement is not a retreat; it is a rediscovery. A rediscovery of yourself, your passions, and the endless possibilities that await you. Who says you can't start a hobby at 65? Or travel to a country you've never even heard of? Or become your grandchildren's most followed influencer on TikTok? (Okay, maybe that last one's a little presumptuous, but who can say no to a little healthy fun?)

Next adventures are at your fingertips. You can explore hidden corners of your neighborhood, learn a new language, or simply rediscover the joy of a sunrise walk. There is no limit to what you can do, except what you set for yourself.
So, as you close this book, I hope you do so with a smile and the enthusiasm of a child who has just received a ticket to an amusement park. Life has given you a new ticket, and it's time to use it!

And remember, every day is a chance to start something new. So, my friend, as I say goodbye and thank you for sharing these pages with me, I encourage you to look forward with curiosity and passion.
After all, "the end" is only a concept. Your next chapter is about to begin. And I am looking forward to reading your story.
Have a great adventure!

A Tip of the Hat and Your Two Cents

Dear esteemed reader and newfound adventurer,

As the final words of this book whisper to a close, I tip my hat to you for journeying through the pages with the zest of a sprightly youngster chasing fireflies at twilight. If laughter bubbled up from your belly or a spark of inspiration kindled in your heart, then my dear friend, we've shared more than mere words — we've shared mirth and camaraderie.

Should the spirit move you, and you find yourself with a nugget or two of fondness for our shared escapades, consider bestowing a kindness upon this humble scribe. A few penned thoughts from your journey might just light the way for another to embark on their own chapter of discovery.
I won't suggest you shout from the rooftops — unless that tickles your fancy — but perhaps a gentle nudge in the form of a shared experience could guide a fellow sojourner.

Let your voice echo in the halls of fellow readers. A swift scan of the QR code below, and you may impart your wisdom and merriment to kindred spirits.

Yours in gratitude and with a wink and a smile,
Bobby Sunray

XX. Uncover the Treasure

Ah, my intrepid explorer of life's golden horizon, you've traversed the chapters as an experienced sailor rides the waves. And here we are, at what you might think is the end, but as with treasure maps and stories of yore, there's a hidden gem tucked away in the last fold.

Behold, the *Retiree's Guide to Online Safety* - a veritable treasure trove of wisdom for navigating the cyber seas. You'll find the treasure map in the form of a quaint QR code; scan it with the magnifying glass of your modern gizmo, be it a smartphone or tablet, and download the file. Lo and behold, the guide is yours to flip through on screen or, for those who prefer the feel of paper between their fingers, to print out.

This guide is your compass to cyber safety, a tome that can be read with the ease of a Sunday morning, giving you peace of mind as you embark on your digital adventures. And don't worry about the rigors of technology; with this guide, you'll be as savvy as a teenager, minus the youthful folly, of course.

So charge your device or warm up the printer, and let the journey continue. Your next chapter is just a QR code away - may it be as compelling and rewarding as the stories of your life so far.
Happy digital adventuring!

Printed in Great Britain
by Amazon